Deleuze and the Schizoanalysis of Cinema

CW00504550

Also available from Continuum:

Deleuze: A Guide for the Perplexed, Claire Colebrook
Deleuze and Guattari's Philosophy of History, Jay Lampert
Deleuze and the Unconscious, Christian Kerslake
Who's Afraid of Deleuze and Guattari?, Gregg Lambert
Deleuze and the Schizoanalysis of Cinema, Ian Buchanan and
Patricia MacCormack

Deleuze and the Schizoanalysis of Cinema

Edited by
Ian Buchanan
and
Patricia MacCormack

continuum

Continuum International Publishing Group

The Tower Building	80 Maiden Lane
11 York Road	Suite 704
London SE1 7NX	New York NY 10038

www.continuumbooks.com

British Library Cataloguing-in-Publication Data
A catalogue record for this book is available from the British Library.

ISBN-10: HB: 1-8470-6127-3
       PB: 1-8470-6128-1
ISBN-13: HB: 978-1-8470-6127-0
       PB: 978-1-8470-6128-7

Library of Congress Cataloguing-in-Publication Data
A catalog record for this book is available from the Library of Congress.

Deleuze and the schizoanalysis of cinema/[edited by] Ian Buchanan and Patricia MacCormack.
   p.cm.
   ISBN 978-1-84706-127-0 – ISBN 978-1-84706-128-7
   1. Motion pictures–Psychological aspects. 2. Deleuze, Gilles, 1925–1995. I. Buchanan, Ian, 1969- II. MacCormack, Patricia. III. Title.

PN1995. D3968 2008
791. 4301′9- -dc22

2008001211

Typeset by Newgen Imaging Systems Pvt Ltd, Chennai, India
Printed and bound in Great Britain by Cromwell Press Ltd, Trowbridge, Wiltshire

For Negar Mottahedeh
For Mark Ferelli

Contents

Contributors

Ian Buchanan is Professor of Critical and Cultural Theory at Cardiff University. He is the founding editor of *Deleuze Studies*.

Gregory Flaxman is an Assistant Professor of English and Comparative Literature. The editor of *The Brain Is the Screen: Deleuze and the Philosophy of Cinema* (U. Minnesota Press, 2000), he is currently finishing a book on philosophy, art and fabulation.

Amy Herzog is Assistant Professor of Media Studies at Queens College, CUNY, where she teaches courses on film theory and popular music. Her work has appeared in American Music and Invisible Culture, and she has contributed essays to edited volumes on music video, on film adaptations of Carmen and a forthcoming collection on Deleuze and cinema. She is currently writing a book that explores the intersections of Deleuzian philosophy and questions of temporality, history and embodiment in musical film.

Joe Hughes recently finished a PhD thesis on the problem of genesis in Deleuze's philosophy at the University of Edinburgh. He is also the co-translator of Deleuze's 'Pericles and Verdi' to be published by Columbia University Press in 2008.

Gregg Lambert is Professor of English, Syracuse University, USA. Among his other writings on the philosophy of Deleuze are *Who's Afraid of Deleuze and Guattari?* (Continuum, 2006) and *The Non-Philosophy of Gilles Deleuze* (Continuum, 2002). He is an advisory editor of Deleuze Connections and a co-editor of *Deleuze Studies*.

Patricia MacCormack is senior lecturer in Communication and Film at Anglia Ruskin University, Cambridge. She has published extensively in the areas of the visceral dimension of cinema, corporeality, the post-human, queer theory, feminism, ethics and continental philosophy. Recent work on perversion, masochism, body modification, non-human rights, Polysexuality and the ethics of becomings have appeared in *Body and Society, Women: A Cultural Review, Thirdspace, Rhizomes and Theory Culture and Society.* Her book *Cinesexuality* is forthcoming from Ashgate.

David Martin-Jones is lecturer in Film Studies at The University of St Andrews, Scotland. He is the author of *Deleuze, Cinema and National Identity* (Edinburgh UP, 2006) and co-author of *Why Deleuze?* (I. B.Tauris, forthcoming). He is also on the editorial board of the international salon-journal, *Film-Philosophy.* His research primarily focuses on Deleuze and cinema, but also examines representations of Scotland, and various Asian Cinemas.

Elena Oxman is a PhD candidate in the department of English and Comparative Literature at the University of North Carolina, Chapel Hill. She is currently finishing her dissertation on the relationship between cinema and thought in French film-philosophy.

Patricia Pisters is professor of film studies at the department of Media Studies of the University of Amsterdam. Her publications include: *Micropolitics of Media Culture: Reading the Rhizomes of Deleuze and Guattari* (ed., Amsterdam University Press, 2001), *The Matrix of Visual Culture: Working with Deleuze in Film Theory* (Stanford University Press, 2003) and *Shooting the Family: Transnational Media and Intercultural Values* (ed. with Wim Staat; Amsterdam University Press, 2005). Her recent articles include: 'Arresting the Flux of Images and Sounds: Free Indirect Discourse and the Dialectics of Political Cinema' in Ian Buchanan and Adrian Parr (eds), *Deleuze and the Contemporary World* (Edinburgh UP, 2006) and 'The Spiritual Dimension of the Brain as Screen. Zigzagging from Cosmos to Earth (and Back')'. In Robert Pepperell (ed.), *Screen Consciousness: Cinema, Mind and World,* Amsterdam and New York: Rodopi.

Anna Powell is author of *Deleuze and the Horror Film* (2005), and has published articles on Deleuze and cinematic affect in *Pli* and *Spectator.* Her latest book *Deleuze, Altered States and Film* is in production with Edinburgh University Press. She is the director of *A/V* (Actual/Virtual) the audio–visual Deleuze Studies webjournal.

Bill Marshall is Professor of Modern French Studies at the University of Glasgow. His publications include book-length studies of the French gay theorist Guy Hocquenghem (1996) and film director André Téchiné (2007), and on Quebec National Cinema (2001).

Mark Riley is a lecturer in Photography and Art History at Roehampton University London. He graduated from Central School of Art and Design in 1985, completed an MA in Fine Art at Central St Martins College of Art and Design in 1997, and a PhD at Goldsmiths College in 2005.

Introduction

Five Theses of Actually Existing Schizoanalysis of Cinema

Ian Buchanan

At a recent dinner party I was told the following joke which I think neatly summarizes the dilemma one faces in trying to answer a question such as the one I have set myself here, namely 'What is a schizoanalysis of cinema?'. A mathematician, an engineer and an accountant are each asked to answer a simple question – what does two plus two equal? The mathematician immediately replies that two plus two equals exactly four. The engineer flips out his calculator and punches away at the keypad for a few minutes and then with great hesitation says two plus two is approximately equal to four. The accountant meanwhile moves closer to the questioner and whispers in their ear, 'what do you want it to be?'. I do not believe the mathematician's certitude, not to mention their exactitude, is available to us: one can safely say Deleuze and Guattari's work has consistency, but not constancy – concepts change their meaning between books, indeed sometimes within books. Do they not themselves say that the inexact is in fact the only truly exact form? This would seem to place us squarely in the engineer's domain. But the engineer's practical concern with materiality (the tensile strength of steel, its rate of decomposition under stress and so forth) which enables him to construct bridges that don't collapse into rivers isn't shared by Deleuze and Guattari. They are indifferent to materiality – it doesn't matter to them if an artwork disintegrates almost as soon as it is made, so long as its production was an event; similarly they don't care if a schizophrenic boy's energy circuit cannot actually conduct electricity. Are we left then with the apparently fraudulent position of the accountant? Yes, but in a very precise sense: the accountant works with constantly changing machines (tax laws) designed to both produce and suppress desire with a view towards finding a way for individuals and corporations to connect to those machines and create for themselves something Guattari called in his last works 'Universes of possibility'. The accountant is as precise as the mathematician and as practical as the engineer, but is creative as well and this it seems to me is how we should approach Deleuze and Guattari's work.[1]

It is reasonable, I suppose, to think that in his two volumes on cinema Deleuze said all that he wanted to say about films and that if he left anything out it was because it was beyond the scope of the strictly philosophical framework he legislated for himself. But even if this is true, and I suspect in a certain way it is, that doesn't mean we have to follow Deleuze in ignoring the questions he left unasked and unanswered, which were neither small nor inconsequential. I'm thinking particularly of the interrelated questions of why we watch certain films and just as significantly why we are willing to pay money to do so, which are central to any understanding of cinema from what Deleuze himself would call a materialist point of view. Deleuze tends to take both these questions for granted, undoubtedly (and quite reasonably, I hasten to add) because his interest lies elsewhere. Consequently, though, his account of cinema is for all its brilliance rather dry, more a catalogue of effects than a full-blooded explanation of how the cinematic machine works. Ironically, perhaps, the expectation that it should or could have been otherwise is aroused by the books on schizoanalysis he wrote with Félix Guattari just prior to his treatises on films. It is in many ways surprising that Deleuze did not draw on this work himself in writing his cinema books because they are a rich resource for thinking through and working out questions to do with the cultural significance and indeed function of cinema. It may be, as Deleuze himself implies, that he needed *not* to do that, in order to 'catch his breath' again after the self-annihilating intensity of his collaboration with Guattari, but it was also in a certain sense unnecessary (Deleuze, 2006: 240). There is nothing to stop us as readers from joining the dots ourselves and putting these apparently separate projects into 'communication' with one another, to use Guattari's phrase (Guattari, 1995a: 138). This is, in effect, the gambit of the present volume: it opens up a range of questions about the study of film Deleuze's cinema books do not engage with directly or do so only tangentially and attempts to answer them by mobilizing concepts drawn from his other works, particularly *Anti-Oedipus* and *A Thousand Plateaus*. The net result of this experiment is a provisional sketching out of a something that can be called a schizoanalysis of cinema.

So what is a schizoanalysis of cinema? There is no simple answer to this question. But in trying to think through what such a thing as a schizoanalysis of cinema might be I take inspiration from one of the great theoretical pioneers in film studies, namely Christian Metz, whose work was among the first to try to demonstrate both the plausibility and possibility of applying psychoanalysis to film. Metz argues that under the conditions of capitalist production cinema contrives to produce itself as a love object (i.e. something that we would willingly pay money to see) and therefore psychoanalysis – as the discourse of the constitution of love objects – is perfectly suited to the task of analysing film. The question of why we pay money to watch films could only be answered, Metz thought, in terms of films' effect on audiences. Metz assumed this effect was the production of meaning and it is this that he set out to explain, using all the resources then available to him (i.e. Lacanian-inflected, structuralist semiotics). It is true that Deleuze distances himself from psychoanalysis and semiotics as well as Metz in the cinema books, but the problem of how films affect us is not as alien to his project as it might at first seem. His taxonomy of image types is simultaneously a catalogue of cinematic effects, the difference being that rather than conceive these effects in terms of meaning as Metz does, he conceives them in terms of sense. But unlike Metz, Deleuze refuses to draw any conclusions from his analysis of the sense of cinema about issues that in his view do not pertain directly to cinema as a specific form of art. He quite explicitly rules out any approach to cinema that either borrows concepts developed in other fields or attempts to go beyond what he regards as the discrete realm of films. He admits that one can 'link framing to castration, or close-ups to partial-objects', for example, but rejects such moves because he cannot 'see what that tells us about cinema' (Deleuze, 1995: 58). Metz is an inspiration because he refuses to treat cinema in so isolated a fashion and approaches it as a stratified artform indissociable from its technical, industrial and ideological support.

If I uphold Metz as a model for the kind of analysis of cinema that I favour it is not with a view to suggesting that Deleuze should somehow have been more like Metz, nor indeed to suggest that we ought to go back to Metz and forget about Deleuze. The former would be absurd and the latter regressive. Regardless of the actual deficiencies of his method, improvised as it was from a not always happy combination of Marxism, psychoanalysis and semiotics, Metz's work remains valuable as a model, I think, because he is one of the few film theorists (and probably the first) who tries to engage with cinema as a whole. It is that ambition – *to engage with cinema as a whole* – which a schizoanalysis of cinema should, in my view, try to fulfil, even at the cost of doing violence to Deleuze's thought. As is well known, Deleuze's cinema project obeys the self-imposed dictum that the 'concepts philosophy introduces to deal with cinema must be specific, must relate specifically to cinema' (Deleuze, 1995: 58). From this perspective, it might be thought that a schizoanalysis of cinema is possible only to the extent that Deleuze's own views on how cinema should be theorized are ignored. This is only partly true. Deleuze was never under any illusion as to the truly heterogeneous nature of cinema and was quite willing to concede that cinematic aesthetics cannot be divorced from what he regarded as 'complementary' questions (e.g. the problem of the ongoing cretinization of cinema, particularly exemplified by rock videos in Deleuze's view) (Deleuze, 1995: 60). If he rejected Metz, it wasn't because Metz concerned himself with such issues, but because his methods weren't sound in Deleuze's view. Deleuze clearly decided at the outset of his project that in order to come to grips with what is specifically filmic about film he had to bracket out such questions as being essentially peripheral to his principal concern. Yet, if Deleuze's own work is taken as a whole, it is difficult to see how such questions as why we desire to watch particular films and willingly pay money to do so are alien to his project. Thus, the first proposition I want to make concerning the schizoanalysis of cinema is that *in order to engage with cinema as a whole we need to take Deleuze as a whole.*

The idea of taking Deleuze 'as a whole' is of course consistent with his own way of doing philosophy, as his comments on how to read Foucault readily attest, but what this means in practice is by no means straightforward (Deleuze, 1995: 84–5). So, I want to make a second proposition: Deleuze's exclusion of questions to do with audience reception, technical development, industrial and commercial process, *should be seen as enabling.* It is the price he has to pay in order to be able to say something precise about how the filmic image functions. The only question is whether or not Deleuze pays too high a price for this precision. There is evidence to suggest Deleuze feared as much himself. Like so many returns of the repressed, issues to do with technical development (especially the advent of sound, but also the transition from black and white to colour), the studio system (particularly with respect to Orson Welles – e.g. his loss of artistic control over the final cut of *The Magnificent Ambersons*), censorship, even money and politics, crop up periodically throughout the two volumes of the cinema books, making it clear Deleuze was both aware of the complexity of cinema as an 'industrial art' and to a certain extent anxious about it as well. Despite his occasional unease, Deleuze never swerves from his determination to extract cinema's concepts and he never permits any of these complementary concerns to take centre-stage. The price he pays for this consistency, however, is that he is unable to explain why this movie and not that movie got made, why this actor and not that one got the lead, why this movie made money and that one didn't and so on and so on. Sparing himself any such concern, he rules that these questions are irrelevant from the perspective of the filmic object as such. 'The cinema', Deleuze says, 'is always as perfect as it can be, taking into account the images and signs which it invents and which it has at its disposal at a given moment' (Deleuze, 1986: x). In one breath he effectively consigns to the dustbin all questions to do with advances in movie-making technology, such as the development of special effects, studio bureaucracy, film-financing, the advent of new distribution systems such as the internet and so on. He not only throws a blanket over the *real politick* of film-making, but also excludes from consideration the vast majority of films made, which in Deleuze's highly ascetic view are drowned in nullity (Deleuze, 1989: 164).

Focused on the exceptions to this rule of a generalized nullity, Deleuze's anatomy of cinema confirms this judgement by making apparent the real degree to which this artform (above all others, perhaps) is reliant on what he disparagingly referred to in a previous book as 'bare repetition', a kind of mechanical repetition which does not yield difference but returns over and over again to an originating structure (Freud's notion of the pleasure principle is a typical example) (Deleuze, 1994: 17). This is precisely his concern when he asks, worriedly: 'What becomes of Hitchcock's suspense, Eisenstein's shock and Gance's sublimity when they are taken up by mediocre authors?' (Deleuze, 1989: 164; cf. 1995: 128–9). Although it is rarely emphasized, this dualism structures Deleuze's entire account of cinema – everywhere he looks he sees bland or bare repetition interrupted by occasional flashes of genuine originality. Indeed, his entire aesthetics is similarly constructed.[2] His interpretation of the works of Francis Bacon is exemplary in this regard. The artist's primary task, Deleuze argues, is to make a space for art by creating the means of dealing with the manifold givens awaiting them in their heads and on the canvas itself. 'We are besieged by photographs that are illustrations, by newspapers that are narrations, by cinema-images, by television-images. There are psychic clichés just as there are physical clichés – ready-made perceptions, memories, phantasms' (Deleuze, 2003: 87). This is why Bacon has to blank out significant portions of the images he paints, it's his way of dealing with the perennial problem of cliché (Deleuze, 2003: 94). Philosophy itself, according to Deleuze, is confronted with a comparable obstacle in the form of opinion, which it has to find the means of circumventing or else wind up similarly mired in the gelatinous morass of the given (Deleuze and Guattari, 1994: 206). Opinion, I would venture, is Deleuze's codeword for commodification in Debord's sense of the word in which its final form is that of the image itself. 'The philosophy of communication', Deleuze writes, by which he means the work of Habermas, but also people like Rawls and

Rorty, 'is exhausted in the search for a universal liberal opinion as consensus, in which we find again the cynical perceptions and affections of the capitalist himself' (Deleuze and Guattari, 1994: 146). Like the Frankfurt School authors before him, and this is not the only point of similarity as we will see in a moment, Deleuze holds that the normal condition of both art and philosophy is defined by the overwhelming presence of the commodification process, but in contrast to them he concentrates on those works which somehow 'escape' that process and determine their own path.

This brings me to my third and, to my mind, most important proposition: *we need to read Deleuze in reverse,* as it were, and emphasize those works which do not escape the commodification process, thus making the schizoanalysis of film a matter of the rule rather than the exception. But having said that, and this is my fourth proposition, I also want to suggest that Deleuze's exceptionalist anatomy of the cinematic image is *the condition of possibility* for just such a schizoanalysis of cinema. This may appear counterintuitive, but as I will argue in more detail below Deleuze's emphasis on the unique is not merely a matter of aesthetics – his way of determining the difference between good and bad works of art and indeed good and bad philosophy – it is the basis of his politics too. However, as a formalist, his first instinct is always to identify the machinic elements that enable as well as constitute a particular work of art. As we've seen, Deleuze is well aware that the shock of an innovation never endures; its force is inevitably appropriated by imitators who give it a second life as 'technique'. But, Deleuze and Guattari insist, 'a work of art is never produced by or for the sake of technique' (Deleuze and Guattari, 1994: 192). Technique concerns materials not composition and in that respect lies outside of Deleuze's conception of the aesthetic. It may be the case that every auteur constructs their action-image in their own way, but the end result is nonetheless still yet another action-image, each repetition a little more banal than the previous. Cinema, in this sense, is more often mechanical than it is machinic, inclined more towards reproduction than production, this being – as Walter Benjamin (1968) argued – what distinguishes it as a twentieth-century artform. Deleuze's inspired abstractions enable us to see this recurrence at the level of form by cutting through the clutter and clamour of the concrete differences between films. What he offers in effect is a kind of ethology of the image, the image reduced to its minimum number of 'affects' or operative elements.[3] But it is an ethology of a very restricted variety since it does not take into consideration what might be termed the image's 'habitat', namely the practical reality of film-making – advances in technology, availability of finance, distribution networks. Yet having said that, it is an ethology focused on the effect of the image and that is its strength.

For Deleuze, cinema is mediocre in its output compared to its potential, as glimpsed in the all-too-infrequent flashes of brilliance found in the works of the great auteurs like Bergman, Hitchcock, Kurosawa and Welles. This judgement is not primarily aesthetic, even if it manifests itself as such, but political. But that, he insists, is no reason to abandon this line of thinking. 'One cannot object by pointing to the vast proportion of rubbish in cinematographic production – it is no worse than anywhere else, although it does have unparalleled economic and industrial consequences' (Deleuze, 1986: xiv). What concerns Deleuze is whether or not cinema as an artform is capable of realizing socially progressive ends – to put it even more bluntly, whether by power of its ability to shock and jolt us it is capable of changing the world for the better as its first theorists and practitioners were certain that it could. But he is also a realist on this matter. 'Everyone knows that, if an art necessarily imposed the shock or vibration, the world would have changed long ago, and men would have been thinking for a long time. So this pretension of the cinema, at least among the greatest pioneers, raises a smile today' (Deleuze, 1989: 157). Ultimately, it is not the mediocrity of cinema that worries Deleuze most, but rather – and here we hear the echo of the Frankfurt School once more – its descent into 'state propaganda and manipulation, into a kind of fascism which brought together Hitler and Hollywood, Hollywood and Hitler. The spiritual automaton became fascist man' (Deleuze, 1989: 164). As Goebbels himself is reputed to have said, fascists obey a law they are not consciously aware of but can recite in their dreams (cited in Virilio, 1994: 11). This development, more than any other, in Deleuze's view spelled the death-knell of cinema's chiliastic ambitions. The production in us of a spiritual automaton – which might be defined simply as an awareness of the power to think, provided it is understood that it is not 'us' who thinks but an 'other' 'at the back of our heads whose age is neither ours nor that of our childhood, but a little time in a pure state' (Deleuze, 1989: 169) – is one of cinema's special powers.[4] Therefore, its corruption, its seemingly helpless degeneration into fascism, is for Deleuze a problem of world-historical proportions, but he nonetheless holds cinema to a higher standard and believes it is capable of better things.

It is true that bad cinema (and sometimes good) limits itself to a dream state induced in the viewer, or – as has been the subject of frequent analysis – to an imaginary participation. But the essence of cinema – which is not the majority of films – has thought as its higher purpose, nothing but thought and its functioning. (Deleuze, 1989: 168)

Psychoanalysis oscillates between these two options and thus, in Deleuze's view, never comes into contact with the real of cinema: it either pretends that what's on screen is a pseudo-dream or it assumes that to enjoy a film the viewer must somehow insert themselves into the drama by identifying with one of its protagonists, but either way it emphasizes the imaginary and the symbolic at the expense of the real. More generally, looking at cinema from the schizoanalytic view of things I have sketched so far, there are three problems with the psychoanalytic approach, which I'll briefly list: first, it fails to treat films as a whole, it concerns itself only with the image on screen; second, it treats the relation to film as transactional, it assumes cinema gives us something, usually pleasure, in exchange for our money; third, it assumes that we do not know why we like cinema – save for the most obviously voyeuristic aspects of it – because it operates on our unconscious not our conscious. My implication is of course that schizoanalysis can and does satisfy the demands this critique of psychoanalysis makes, but first we have to attend to the issue of the nature of the cinematic object. This brings me to my fifth and final proposition: *cinema is delirium.*[5] Essentially, what Deleuze and Guattari argue in *Anti-Oedipus* is this: the schizophrenic, in the full flight of delirium, reveals to us the true nature of desire as a synthetic process. Delirium, then, is Deleuze and Guattari's model of how desire works. 'Before being a mental state of the schizophrenic who has made himself into an artificial person through autism, schizophrenia is the process of the production of desire and desiring-machines' (Deleuze and Guattari, 2004: 26). Cinema, by extension, is the production of desiring-machines. But Deleuze doesn't say this in so many words. Rather he argues that cinema's purpose as an artform is the engendering of ideas, but I want to argue that his implication is that when it fails to produce ideas it leaves us with a heterogeneous muddle of desiring-machines.

According to Deleuze, cinema doesn't make thought visible, instead it brings us face-to-face with thought's impossibility and in that way induces thought in the very place it had been absent. But it is only able to do this to the extent that it breaks with the structures of what Deleuze calls the movement-image, which in this context might be defined as cinema's power of common-sense, but it can also be regarded as its innate tendency towards fascism.[6] Deleuze's 'natural history' of the cinema is divided into two distinct phases in which two very different image-regimes hold sway.[7] The first phase, designated the movement-image because cinema's distinctiveness as an artform derives from the fact that it is a self-moving image, takes us from the birth of cinema to the end of World War II, when in Deleuze's view it was aesthetically exhausted; the second phase, designated the time-image because at this point cinema realized its true vocation, namely the production of segments of pure time, takes us from World War II until the present. In cinema's first phase, what was seen on screen was organized according to the dictates of what Deleuze calls the 'sensory-motor scheme', which orients the image around a perception-action couplet. Its primary effect is to contain the inherent delirium of the cinematic image, which Deleuze implies stems from the way the 'screen, as the frame of frames, gives a common standard of measurement to things which do not have one – long shots of countryside and close-ups of the face, an astronomical system and a single drop of water – parts which do not have the same denominator of distance, relief or light. In all these senses the frame ensures a deterritorialisation of the image' (Deleuze, 1986: 14–15).[8] Outside of the darkened confines of the theatre only the seriously deranged could make the kinds of global comparisons routinely constructed by the cinematic image. By imbuing the image with a logical causality it acts as a kind of 'shock defence' (to use Benjamin's adaptation of Freud's term) against the deterritorializing power of the image, which is not de-realizing as psycho-analysis suggests, but its opposite, the opening up of a space in which the impossible becomes the merely improbable (Benjamin, 1973: 114–17).

The distinctiveness of the 'sensory-motor scheme' as an image-regime and indeed its limitations became apparent – in true Hegelian fashion, I might add – after the owl of Minerva had taken flight, when its successor the time-image first made its appearance in the work of the Italian neo-realists, particularly De Sica and Rossellini. Now the full potential for the delirium of the image was exploited. The bombed-out landscapes of Rossellini's early films *Open City* (1945) and *Germany: Year Zero* (1947) presented a new kind of cinema in which setting was no longer directly invested by action, but instead imparted its own kind of affect. Moreover, Rossellini populated his films with strange characters with no bearing on the central drama, further weakening the hegemony of the sensory-motor scheme. 'In the old realism or on the model of the action-image [one of three main avatars of the movement-image], objects and setting already had a reality of their own, but it was a functional reality, strictly determined by the demands of the situation, even if these demands were as much poetic as dramatic.' But with neo-realism, 'objects and settings [*milieux*] take on an autonomous, material reality which gives them an importance in them-selves' (Deleuze, 1989: 4). Now, for viewer and character alike, the setting is invested by the gaze and the very notion of what constitutes a situation changes – it becomes purely optical and auditory. Perception no longer automatically connects to action, the glint of light off a knife's edge no longer means a stabbing is about to occur, but might have a more meta-phorical or even lyrical purpose. This new type of situation is not induced by an action, nor can it be resolved with an action. Instead, it 'makes us grasp, it is supposed to make us grasp, something intolerable and unbear-able' (Deleuze, 1989: 18) – life on a knife's edge. This intolerable something is not a matter of brute violence or terror, but rather 'something too power-ful, or too unjust, but sometimes also too beautiful' (Deleuze, 1989: 18). Deleuze goes on to draw an ethical distinction between the two different image-regimes:

> The important thing [in the time-image] is always that the character or viewer, and the two together, become visionaries. The purely optical and sound situation gives rise to a seeing function, at once fantasy and report, criticism and compassion, whilst sensory-motor situations, no matter how violent, are directed to a pragmatic visual function which 'tolerates' or 'puts up with' practically anything, from the moment it becomes involved in a system of actions and reactions. (Deleuze, 1989: 19)

Philosophy itself, in Deleuze's view, has no higher calling than this, the identification of the intolerable. I would go so far as to say that for Deleuze philosophy exists for no other purpose, as is patent in his interest – most directly articulated in *Anti-Oedipus* – in the matter of voluntary servitude, the apparently inexplicable willingness on the part of many to put up with and indeed tolerate the intolerable. Paradoxically, then, cinema's excep-tionalism when it is achieved is expressed in its ability to make apparent the rule, that which is customary rather than that which is unusual. When it fails, however, it gives us nothing but fantasy, the million and one private exceptions to the rule that lack both truth and reality. Here Deleuze antici-pates Badiou's critique of postmodernity, which similarly rejects particularity (the merely different) in favour of singularity (genuine difference) (Badiou, 2006: 134). But Deleuze is less pessimistic than Badiou, who regards con-temporary cinema as a form of sterile neo-classicism that does nothing except recycle old stories, old images and old ideas (Badiou, 2005: 123). Deleuze would probably have no qualms about rejecting the bulk of con-temporary cinema as cretinizing schlock as Badiou does, but would no doubt want to add that such judgements are of little use. They don't help us to understand cinema any better. So rather than moralize about the vacuity of Hollywood, I expect Deleuze would instead have us continue to sift the dross in search for that rare nugget of innovation. In this sense, Jameson is surely correct to describe Deleuze as a modernist, but it is for precisely that reason that we need to *reverse* Deleuze and look not at the exceptions to the rule of a generalized nullity in cinema he identifies, but at that nullity itself – sexploitation films, blaxploitation films, direct to video shockers, sequels and prequels, remakes and rip-offs, blockbusters and stinkers, the bread and butter of Hollywood, the stuff on which the industry was founded and sustains itself (Jameson, 2002: 4). Nowhere does Deleuze write about *Hell Behind Bars, Shaft, Night of the Living Dead, The Birds 2*, or even *Star Wars* (which when he wrote his cinema books was the highest grossing film of all time), yet this is *real* Hollywood. The question before us, clearly enough, is what does *this* kind of cinema do? How does *it* work?

Not only doesn't Deleuze answer this question in his cinema books, he constructs an aesthetic binary that places such uninspiring cinema beyond the pale. Cinema produces a spiritual automaton that is the one universal 'effect' of the medium Deleuze allows. Spinoza calls this anonymous something, this 'it', that thinks in us the soul. When it is working well, when it is good, that spiritual automaton has a liberating effect on our subjectivity; but when it isn't working well, when it is bad, then that spiritual automaton tends to be enslaving. If the spiritual automaton is an awareness of the power to think, then liberation means an increase in the power to think, which could be defined as a power of differentiation; while enslavement clearly means the opposite, a diminution in the power to think, which could be defined as a tendency towards sameness or, what amounts to the same thing, bad non-differentiating repetition. What this means philosophically becomes clearer if we connect it to Deleuze's account of the Spinozist origins of the concept of spiritual automaton. 'What was lacking in the ancients, says Spinoza, was the conception of the soul as a sort of spiritual automaton, that is, of thought as determined by its own laws' (Deleuze, 1990: 160). The spiritual automaton is an idea, or mode of thought, that is caused by and in thought itself. It is thus a 'true' idea, or an 'adequate' idea, because it knows and expresses its own cause. Its opposite is the 'sad passion', the thought or idea that doesn't know its own cause. Sad passions obstruct our ability to act.[9] If we react to what we see on screen, if we are affected by what we see, then by definition our response cannot be considered an adequate idea because it was caused by something outside of thought. Our laughter or tears in response to a film are 'sad passions' because they are unaware of their own causes. It is only when cinema induces thought, when it yields an idea, suggested but not caused by what occurs on screen, that we can consider it to have produced a 'truth effect' (to borrow Badiou's useful term). Deleuze's entire 'natural history' of cinema can be understood, then, as charting a passage from a cinema of 'sad passions' – that is, a cinema driven by the aim of producing an affect – to a cinema of 'adequate ideas'.[10]

There is a two-fold problem with this approach to cinema. First, if as Deleuze readily admits the bulk of cinema doesn't realize the artform's true purpose of producing ideas, then an analysis that is only interested in ideas isn't going to tell us all that much about the majority of films made. Second, if we accept Deleuze's thesis that only rare films produce ideas of the spiritual automaton type, it doesn't necessarily follow that those films which fail in this endeavour are either cretinizing or worse fascisizing, yet these are effectively the only options Deleuze's cinema aesthetics leaves us with. Deleuze's decision to treat films philosophically means he treats it as an artform constructed in his own image. He finds philosophy in film because that's what he is looking for, which isn't to say that film cannot contain philosophy, but it is to question whether or not philosophy should be the principle focus of analysis. I am not suggesting we need to abandon the philosophical approach to cinema Deleuze advocates, but I am saying it needs to be supplemented by an analysis – a schizoanalysis – of the dimensions of cinema that do not pertain to the production of ideas, namely those that pertain to desire and to interest, and this, I want to argue, is the signal advantage of a schizoanalysis of cinema over existing forms of film analysis: by mobilizing the problematic of desire it enables us to inject fresh life into old questions, namely those relating to what I have called the real conditions of production, which for the most part seem to be stuck permanently on the plane of self-evidence known as 'marketing' wherein it is *known* that movies like the *X-men* trilogy get made because it is a *fact* that teenage boys are the predominant audience demographic – by a large margin – in both the cinema-goer and video-renter markets.[11] Therefore it is *their* tastes that dictate what is deemed marketable and worth spending a couple of hundred million dollars to make and what isn't.[12] But this doesn't explain why, stereotypically, teenage boys appear to desire movies of that type; nor indeed, given the vast number of box-office bombs made in pursuit of this particular market, does it reliably tell what they actually desire.[13]

In the final section of *Anti-Oedipus*, Deleuze and Guattari specify that in establishing schizoanalysis there are three tasks that must be performed: one negative task, and two positive tasks. To begin with, 'schizoanalysis goes by way of destruction – a whole scouring of the unconscious, a complete curettage' (Deleuze and Guattari, 2004: 342). What must be destroyed? In Deleuze and Guattari's view nothing less than the entire psychoanalytic inheritance. Oedipus, the ego, the superego, guilt, law, castration, all these things must be rooted out at the source and dispensed with as so much trash. But hyperbole aside, what they mean in analytic terms is this: we need to set aside the idea that desire has an intrinsic script it is supposed to follow and that all pathologies can be attributed to a failure to adhere to its dictates. We are neither sick from our childhood, nor essentially stuck in our childhood. Desire is a synthetic or machinic process with a multiplicity of operating parts and a tremendous power of association or connection which we think only in triangular terms – desire is much more complicated than mommy-daddy-me. It follows, then, that the two positive tasks of schizo-analysis should concentrate on trying to get a grip on desire as it actually is. 'The first positive task consists of discovering in a subject the nature, the formation, or the functioning of *his* desiring-machines, independently of any interpretations. What are your desiring-machines, what do you put into these machines, what is the output, how does it work, what are your nonhuman sexes?' (Deleuze and Guattari, 2004: 354). The second positive task of schizoanalysis consists of reaching 'the investments of unconscious desire of the social field, insofar as they are differentiated from the preconscious investments of interest, and insofar as they are not merely capable of coun-teracting them, but also of coexisting with them in opposite modes' (Deleuze and Guattari, 2004: 383). What they mean by this, simply put, is that desire works by creating mental matrices to trap, interrupt and divert libido and that these matrices (which they call desiring-machines) can encompass matters and flows of every type. That is to say, contrary to Freud, desire can invest the social field directly, and no artform shows the truth of this more clearly than cinema.

How these three tasks should be fulfilled in the context of cinema studies is an open and to my mind extremely interesting question which this volume as a whole can only hope to begin to answer in a very provi-sional way. The five propositions I have offered here are my way of fulfilling these three tasks in relation to Deleuze's own work on cinema. My hope is that this will help clear the way for the bigger task of rethinking cinema studies in general. I must say, too, in introducing a volume like this I cannot possibly speak for everyone, except to say that there is a common project here, albeit one pursued by varying means. I would add that this volume intends neither to be the first word nor the last word on the schizoanalysis of cinema. It is rather a call to action, an attempt to jumpstart a discussion that some of us think is long overdue. As should be clear in the pages that follow, this call to action isn't intended to supplant Deleuze's cinema books with his 'Guattarized' books. On the contrary, we reject this specious segmentation of Deleuze's corpus and instead take seriously Deleuze's demand that we take an author 'as a whole'. The common project here then consists in reading both the schizoanalytic books and the cinema books together with a view towards synthesizing their insights into a new way of thinking about the cinema. We also aim to overturn the misguided and largely self-imposed injunction against interpretation that Deleuzians everywhere seem to feel they must uphold regardless of the fact that there is no basis whatsoever in Deleuze's work to support it. Deleuze and Guattari only say that the unconscious cannot be interpreted, not that interpretation per se is impossible, and what's more their work clearly engages in all kinds of interpretive activity.

Chapter 1

Schizoanalysis and the Phenomenology of Cinema

Joe Hughes

Is a schizoanalysis of cinema possible? That depends on at least two things: what schizoanalysis is and how we interpret Deleuze's study and classification of cinema's signs. On a first reading Deleuze's classification of signs seems to be derived from a careful and comprehensive study of the films themselves. It almost seems as though he constructed a prodigious semiology of cinema, collecting dominant images from the history of film, ordering them and arranging them into groups. An 'icon', for example, is a type of image which expresses an emotion or an affect (1986: 110). Deleuze used the example of Joan's face in Bresson's *The Trial of Joan of Arc*, but the film critic will find other images functioning as icons in other films by other directors across the history of cinema. Such a reading of the cinema books would suggest that Deleuze's work contributes to film studies by helping us understand the language of cinema and the way it speaks to its audience, for example, through its creation and manipulation of emotions.

But on a second reading, this approach to Deleuze's work seems slightly less plausible. As Deleuze makes abundantly clear in the fourth chapter of *Cinema 1*, the set of signs collected in the two books are *not* abstracted and generalized versions of signs populating various canonical films. Instead they refer back to a 'Bergsonian' theory of the subject. Deleuze 'deduces' the structure of this subject from what he calls the 'plane of immanence' (1986: 58). The plane of immanence is the set of all movement-images – images which are themselves indistinguishable from 'matter' – in which each image 'acts on the others and reacts to others on "all their facets at once" and "by all their elements"' (1986: 58). Within this field of matter there is an 'interval' – the 'brain' – in which a 'material subjectivity' is differentiated into three distinct moments of a sensory-motor schema: perception, affection and action (1986: 62).

It is this general structure of material subjectivity which determines cinema's signs. When the material subject 'perceives' the matter distributed across the plane of immanence, that matter is represented in one of three possible signs: a 'dicisign', a 'reume' or a 'gramme'. When those perceptions are extended into affections they become represented in the form of three more signs: 'icons', 'qualisigns' or 'dividuals'. When they are further extended into actions they define even more kinds of signs. In other words the signs that Deleuze discovers in cinema are not abstracted from the collected images of different films. Instead they mark out the different potential experiences of a material subject. When a movement-image is taken up in perception, it yields a dicisign. When it is felt, it yields an icon. From this point of view the cinema books do not so much help us understand the language of cinema as they help us understand the structure of a material subjectivity.

Deleuze introduces a distinction between semiotics and semiology which makes this point even more clearly. 'Semiology' studies sign systems as linguistic systems; 'semiotics' studies non-linguistic, and in this case, phenomenological sign systems (1989: 28–34, 262). Deleuze clearly understands his study to represent a semiotics, not a semiology. What Deleuze is describing in these books is not the language of cinema, as Christian Metz attempted, but the structure and 'language' of a 'non-linguistic' subjectivity. In this essay I trace this theory of subjectivity – at a very formal level – back to two of Deleuze's earlier works: *The Logic of Sense* and, with Guattari, *Anti-Oedipus*. In doing so I hope to achieve two things. First, I want to begin examining this theory of subjectivity which underlies the cinema books. Second, I want to make the case that Deleuze's analysis of cinema is already a schizoanalysis.

Anti-Oedipus

What is schizoanalysis? Deleuze and Guattari give several definitions throughout *Anti-Oedipus*, all of which seem to converge on one: 'Schizoanalysis is at once a transcendental and a materialist analysis. [. . .] It sets out to explore a transcendental unconscious [. . .]' (1983: 109; cf. 75). This is the broadest definition of schizoanalysis that they give. It defines schizoanalysis as the exploration of a material and a transcendental unconscious. But it has several formulations. For example, the 'task of schizoanalysis is that of learning what a subject's desiring-machines are, how they work, with what syntheses, what bursts of energy in the machine, what constituent misfires, with what flows, what chains and what becomings in each case' (1983: 338). 'Desiring-machine', however, is simply an alternate expression for the transcendental unconscious (1983: 26). In asking what schizoanalysis is, then, we are inevitably pushed on to ask a new question: what is a desiring-machine? What exactly is this transcendental unconscious that schizoanalysis sets out to discover and describe?

For Deleuze and Guattari, the transcendental unconscious is a process of production comprising three distinct moments: a connective synthesis, a disjunctive synthesis and a conjunctive synthesis. These three syntheses are '*passive*' syntheses. Deleuze, who first made use of the notion of passive synthesis in *Difference and Repetition*, took the notion from Husserl. Husserl took it from Kant. In the *Critique of Pure Reason* Kant described three transcendental syntheses: 'the synthesis of apprehension in intuition', 'the synthesis of reproduction in the imagination' and 'the synthesis of recognition in the concept'. These three syntheses were intended to mediate sensibility and the understanding. They move from the discontinuity of the sensible manifold to the unity of the concept. The first synthesis surveys and gathers together the moments differentiated in 'inner sense' or the empty form of time. But since this synthesis is itself in time, a second synthesis of reproduction is required to reproduce its representations in the following present. But now there are two different representations: a past present and a present present. A third synthesis is therefore needed in order to recognize the past present and the present present as parts of the same consciousness: 'without consciousness that that which we think is the very same as what we thought a moment before, all reproduction in the series of representations would be in vain' (Kant, 1998: A 103). The third synthesis therefore recognizes that representations produced in the first two syntheses are for one and the same consciousness. In this way the three syntheses move from 'the manifold that has been successively intuited, and then also reproduced, [to] *one* representation' (1998: A 103; my emphasis).

In the first edition of the *Critique* each synthesis was brought about by a specific faculty: 'sense, imagination, and apperception' (1998: A 94/B 127; cf. A 115). Only the third was grounded in spontaneity and operated with the freedom and the self-conscious *activity* which characterized apperception. The first two syntheses belonged to faculties that were *passive* (cf. 1998: B 153). When Kant re-wrote the *Critique*, he famously changed things so that all three syntheses fell under the jurisdiction of the understanding (cf. 1998: B 151). All three syntheses became what Husserl (and Deleuze following him) would call 'active syntheses'. For Husserl this move obscured Kant's 'brilliant insight' into a type of synthesis that operated passively (Husserl, 2001: 410). Anthony Steinbock summarizes these aspects of the notion of passive synthesis as follows:

> Husserl cites the A edition of the *Critique* because Kant speaks of a faculty, the power of imagination, that is independent of the Understanding rather than being subordinate to and a function of the Understanding. Whereas the Understanding has the spontaneous character of *active syntheses* that hold together and connect the sensuous manifold according to rules, sensibility has the character of *passivity*, since the inner and outer sense merely receive sense data. In this case, of course, the expression, 'passive synthesis' is oxymoronic from a Kantian perspective. (Steinbock, 2001: xl)

A passive synthesis is one which takes place without 'rules', without freedom or volition, and under the radar of any sort of unified consciousness. Deleuze manages to fit all of this into one succinct sentence in *Difference and Repetition*: a passive synthesis is a synthesis that 'is not carried out by the mind, but occurs *in* the mind' (1994: 71; original emphasis). It is, you could say, sensory-motor.

The transcendental unconscious of *Anti-Oedipus* is composed of three such syntheses, and the primary task of schizoanalysis is describing these syntheses in detail. But schizoanalysis also makes a second discovery which is even more fundamental and which we have to describe before we can fully understand the role of syntheses. Prior to passive synthesis schizoanalysis discovers a material field of 'partial objects'. Partial objects are the 'ultimate elements of the unconscious' (1983: 324). They represent its material beginnings. These partial objects have two general characteristics both of which will become important below. First, they are small. They are the 'molecules' themselves of a 'molecular unconscious' (1983: 309, 323). Second, they exist in a state of 'positive dispersion in a molecular multiplicity' (1983: 342). 'Positive dispersion' means that the only relation between partial objects is the lack of relation (1983: 314). The three syntheses of the transcendental unconscious will indeed create relations between partial objects, but considered as a 'molecular multiplicity' there are not yet any relations between them. Partial objects exist *independently of the transcendental unconscious which will be built on their foundation.*

The three passive syntheses synthesize these objects. They do not, like Kant's, synthesize the purely formal discontinuities of inner sense or of time. Rather, they synthesize material fragments which function as a sort of hyletic data (1983: 36). They synthesize the content of sensation rather than its form. The first synthesis of 'connection' directly apprehends and gathers together partial objects. It creates initial connections or 'flows' between them (1983: 6). The second synthesis builds on the work of the first. It no longer synthesizes the material partial objects, but reproduces or 'records' the objects apprehended in the first synthesis, thus turning partial objects into 'data' for an unconscious ego: 'The data, the bits of information recorded, and their transmission form a grid of disjunctions of a type that differs from the previous connections' (1983: 38). The third synthesis of conjunction then runs through and gathers together the first synthesis and the second. It attempts a 'genuine reconciliation of the two' (1983: 17). It recognizes the compatibility of the first and the second synthesis, that they are both parts of the same ego. It measures the first against the second and expresses the difference between the two in the form of 'intensities' (1983: 19; cf. 21).

The transcendental unconscious which schizoanalysis unveils therefore has this general form: founded on a field of materiality there are three passive syntheses: (1) a passive synthesis of apprehension, (2) a passive synthesis of reproduction and (3) a passive synthesis of recognition or reconciliation. Schematically, we can organize it like this:

1. Material field
2. First passive synthesis
3. Second passive synthesis
4. Third passive synthesis

The Logic of Sense

The general structure of this 'transcendental unconscious' was already laid out in great detail by Deleuze in *The Logic of Sense*. Deleuze describes *The Logic of Sense* as a 'logical and psychological novel' which tells the story of the genesis of representation (1990: xiv). Within the general story, there are two subplots: a 'dynamic genesis' and a 'static genesis'. The static genesis, with which we are *not* concerned, moves from an *immaterial* transcendental field – the 'virtual' – to an empirical consciousness structured by the form of the proposition (1990: 244). It is a process which usually goes by the name of 'actualisation'. But this genesis and the entire transcendental field on which it is founded presupposes a dynamic genesis. Contrary to the static genesis, the dynamic genesis begins in a *material* field of 'partial objects' and produces the immaterial transcendental field through a series of passive syntheses. If we compare the formal structure of *Anti-Oedipus*'s transcendental unconscious to the moments of this dynamic genesis, we will see that they have very much in common.

First, in *The Logic of Sense*, the dynamic genesis begins with a material field of 'partial objects'. Deleuze gives various names to this field: 'primary order', 'corporeal depth', 'schizophrenic mixture', the 'Id' and so on. But whatever the name, this field is a place in which 'material fragments' or 'partial objects' collide with one another (1990: 187). In the primary order 'everything is body and corporeal. Everything is a mixture of bodies, and inside the body, interlocking and interpenetration' (1990: 87). Bodies 'burst and cause other bodies to burst *in* an universal cesspool' (1990: 187; original emphasis). Just as in *Anti-Oedipus*, an unconscious structured by three passive syntheses will indeed be produced on the foundation of this chaotic material field, but, in itself, this field and the partial objects which populate it, exist independently of that unconscious. In a formulation which clearly resonates with *Cinema 1* through its allusion to *Matter and Memory* Deleuze even goes so far as to say that in this field, '*a body penetrates another and coexists with it in all of its parts, like a drop of wine in the ocean, or fire in iron*' (1990: 5–6; my emphasis). The primary order represents the communication of partial objects among themselves without any reference to a synthesizing unconscious.

Within this mixture of bodies, there is something Deleuze calls the 'ego' or 'the body without organs'. The body without organs, at this point, is nothing other than a power of synthesis – a 'liquid principle' – which brings about a first passive synthesis (1990: 189). It begins to bind or 'weld' the material fragments which 'whirl about and explode' in the corporeal depths (1990: 189; cf. 1990: 87). Deleuze calls this binding the first synthesis of 'connection'. Like the first synthesis of *Anti-Oedipus*, this synthesis directly apprehends the partial objects of the material field, and just as that synthesis produced 'data', this synthesis produces 'partial surfaces' of the body which are nothing other than images of the contemplated partial objects (1990: 197). This leads to a second synthesis of 'conjunction' which gathers together the partial surfaces of the body into a full surface (1990: 200). Here *The Logic of Sense* would seem to break with *Anti-Oedipus*: the second synthesis is now called 'conjunction' rather than 'disjunction'. We should not put too much emphasis on the words, however. In both books the second synthesis has the same *function* and works in the same way. Just as the second synthesis of *Anti-Oedipus* took up and recorded the information apprehended in the first synthesis, the second synthesis of *The Logic of*

Sense takes up and binds together the partial surfaces produced in the first synthesis. Finally, there is a third synthesis of 'disjunction'. Where the third synthesis of *Anti-Oedipus* tried to reconcile the first synthesis with the second, the third synthesis of *The Logic of Sense* tries to reconcile the first synthesis with the second. It is in this third synthesis that the similarities between *Anti-Oedipus* and *The Logic of Sense* really seem to stop.

Before we go on to study the differences between the two accounts of the third synthesis we can note that at the very formal level with which we are concerned here, *Anti-Oedipus* and *The Logic of Sense* are strikingly similar. Both describe the unconscious as a 'process of production' or as a 'genesis'. In both this genesis begins in a material field populated by 'partial objects' or material fragments. In both a first synthesis begins binding these fragments. In both a second synthesis takes over where the first synthesis left off, and in both a third synthesis tries to reconcile the first two syntheses. We can therefore use our schematic representation of *Anti-Oedipus* as a formal description of *The Logic of Sense*:

1. Material field
2. First passive synthesis
3. Second passive synthesis
4. Third passive synthesis

The character of the third passive synthesis is difficult to settle on. In *Anti-Oedipus*, it is relatively straightforward: the third synthesis measures the first against the second and expresses the difference between the two in the form of an intensity. Deleuze and Guattari describe it as a 'reconciliation' of the first two syntheses, and it appears, apparently, a successful reconciliation. In *The Logic of Sense*, however, the third synthesis is a *failed* synthesis. It does indeed begin as an attempt at recognition or reconciliation. But Deleuze calls this initial attempt only the 'intended action' or the image of 'action in general', the action-image (1990: 206). In the first synthesis, the ego passively synthesized partial objects. In the second, it passively synthesized partial surfaces. In the third, the ego intends to continue passively synthesizing, but it is no longer successful. It is not clear what exactly goes wrong in the third synthesis, but it is clear that the intended action is never actually accomplished. The third synthesis therefore has two parts: (1) the 'intended action' and (2) the 'action effectively accomplished' (1990: 207). The action effectively accomplished is the disruption of the sensor-motor structure of passive synthesis in general. The surface of the body that the second passive synthesis created, falls apart and everything is submitted to a new type of synthesis on a 'new metaphysical surface, or surface of pure thought' (1990: 208).

Instead of leading to intensity, the third passive synthesis of *The Logic of Sense* leads to a transcendental surface of thought. Deleuze says something particularly important about this surface which should illuminate our reading of the cinema books. This new surface, the metaphysical surface of thought – or the 'virtual' – is defined by a particular type of time: 'at the incorporeal surface, we recognize the pure line of Aion' (1990: 209; cf. 215). Throughout *The Logic of Sense*, Deleuze opposes two types of temporality: Chronos and Aion. Chronos is the time of bodies and their mixture in the schizophrenic depths of the primary order (1990: 162, 87). Here, time is measured in relation to movement, and the present is the dominant dimension of time. This is why the first genesis of *The Logic of Sense* is called the *dynamic* genesis: it begins in a material field defined primarily by 'movement' or the action and passion of fragmented bodies on one another. In opposition to Chronos, Aion is an immaterial time, time freed from movement, or time in its pure state. It is what Deleuze calls, alluding to Kant, 'the empty form of time', or the form of everything that changes but which does not itself change (1990: 62, 165). In this time of pure thought there is no present, or rather the present is infinitely subdivided into a past and a future. Nothing happens, but everything has already happened and is about to happen.

To summarize the Deleuzian unconscious as it appears in both *Anti-Oedipus* and *The Logic of Sense* we can say that (1) everything begins in a material field of partial objects in which time is subordinated to movement. (2) Three passive syntheses take up and process this primary matter, but in the third synthesis, passivity fails. The sensory-motor structure gives way to a new 'surface' and a new synthesis. (3) This new surface which grows out of the failure of the third passive synthesis represents time in its pure state or the empty form of time. Our schematic representation now looks like this:

1. Material field
2. First passive synthesis
3. Second passive synthesis
4. Third passive synthesis
5. Empty form of time

I want to stress that this is not the entire Deleuzian subject. It is simply its unconscious, passive half. The dynamic genesis leads to a static genesis.

Desiring-production leads to social production. The events populating the empty form of time will eventually be actualized into an empirical consciousness. What I have described here is only the first half of Deleuze's overall theory of subjectivity. These five moments constitute the basic structure of the Deleuzian unconscious.

Cinema 1

These five moments of the Deleuzian unconscious are also the critical moments of the material subjectivity underlying the cinema books. This subjectivity, as I briefly described at the beginning of the essay has five aspects: (1) the plane of immanence from which it is deduced; (2) the perception-image; (3) the affection-image; (4) the action-image and (5) the time-image. Here I want to briefly suggest that each one of these aspects is modelled on moments on the Deleuzian unconscious as it was developed in both *The Logic of Sense* and *Anti-Oedipus*.

The 'plane of immanence' is the field in which 'movement-images' act and react on one another in all their parts and on all their facets (1986: 58–9). But 'the movement-image is matter itself' (1989: 33). The plane of immanence, then, is a field of matter at the foundation of subjectivity in which the material 'images' act and react on one another in all their parts. It is the functional equivalent of both the 'molecular multiplicity of partial objects in positive dispersion' (*Anti-Oedipus*) and of the 'primary order' of schizophrenic and corporeal depths (*The Logic of Sense*). In all three books subjectivity is founded on a material field which is described in the same way: material fragments communicate with one another independently of any subject. In both *The Logic of Sense* and the cinema books, this material field is one in which time is subordinated to movement.

In *Anti-Oedipus* and *The Logic of Sense* a first passive synthesis of apprehension began binding together the material fragments of the plane of immanence. In this act of synthesis a rudimentary ego – the body without organs – contemplates the material field. It takes up the partial objects and transforms them into or bits of data to be recorded or into partial surfaces of the body. Similarly, in the cinema books the first image to be deduced from the plane of immanence is a contemplation of materiality. The 'perception-image' represents the 'brain's' apprehension of the plane of immanence (1986: 62). The brain 'perceives' movement-images and 'frames' them (1986: 63). It therefore has the same function as the synthesis of apprehension in the other two books: it 'perceives' matter.

In *Anti-Oedipus* and *The Logic of Sense* a second synthesis takes over where the first left off. It binds together and 'records' the passing images that the synthesis of apprehension produced. This is also how Deleuze describes the affection-image, or the second passive moment of material subjectivity.

> There is inevitably a part of external movements that we 'absorb', that we refract, and which does not transform into either objects of perception or acts of the subject; rather they mark the coincidence of the subject and the object in a pure quality. (1986: 62)

The affection-image is the retention and the reproduction of 'external movements' or the movement-images of the plane of immanence. It 'absorbs' movement rather than letting it pass. Like the second syntheses of *Anti-Oedipus* and *The Logic of Sense*, it functions as a form of retention and reproduction.

The third synthesis of *The Logic of Sense* had two moments: the intended action and the action effectively accomplished. The first defines the action-image. Like the third synthesis of *Anti-Oedipus*, the action-image is a reconciliation of the first two kinds of images. For Deleuze, action requires two things: first there must be a 'sensory contact' with an object (perception); second, that object 'must, in a way, reawaken an affective memory, reactualize an emotion . . .' (affection) (1986: 158). Action requires perception and affection. It is their synthesis. The 'genetic sign' of the action-image is thus defined by the synthesis of 'object and emotion', of perception and affection (1986: 158). The action-image is the successful synthesis of the first two moments of material subjectivity. It realizes the intended action of *The Logic of Sense*.

But at almost the same time cinema experiences a 'crisis of the action-image' and a failure of its synthesis. The intended action gives way to the action effectively accomplished. In the crisis of the action-image, the sensor-motor link between perception and affection fails. Either perception fails to excite memory, or memory has nothing to contribute to the situation: 'the situation [the character] is in outstrips his motor capacities on all sides, and makes him see and hear what is no longer subject to the rules of a response or an action' (1989: 3). These kinds of images, which are 'no longer subject to the rules of a response', constitute a new type of sign: opsigns and sonsings, pure visual and auditory signs 'which are no longer sensory-motor and which bring the emancipated senses into direct relation with *time and thought*' (1989: 17; my emphasis). They offer 'pure and direct images of time' (1989: 17).

With these new signs we have clearly moved onto the immaterial, metaphysical surface which Deleuze described in *The Logic of Sense*. The time-image represents for us a field of pure thought in which time is no longer subordinated to movement.

> There is becoming, change, passage. But the form of what changes does not itself change, does not pass on. This is time, time itself, 'a little time in its pure state': a direct time-image, which gives what changes the unchanging form in which the change is produced. (1989: 17)

Contrary to the time of the plane of immanence, there is no present moment here. Characters now live 'the pure form of a time which is torn between an already determined past and a dead-end future' (1989: 24; cf. 271).

The history of cinema on Deleuze's reading thus moves from matter to pure thought, from movement to time, but it does so by following the structure of a transcendental unconscious already laid out by Deleuze as early as 1969. The schematic representations we used to highlight the moments of a transcendental unconscious structuring both *Anti-Oedipus* and *The Logic of Sense* can therefore apply to the cinema books as well. A more elaborate version would look like this:

1. Material field   (plane of immanence)
2. First passive synthesis   (perception-image)
3. Second passive synthesis   (affection-image)
4. Third passive synthesis   (action-image)
5. Failure of the third synthesis   (crisis of the action-image)
6. Pure thought, empty time   (pure thought, empty time)

The material subjectivity of *Cinema 1* is a reformulation of the transcendental unconscious of *Anti-Oedipus* and of the dynamic genesis of *The Logic of Sense*. All three are accounts of the same Deleuzian unconscious.

Conclusion

Although this reading is extremely general and necessarily reductive, I think it warrants two similarly broad conclusions, or at least the articulation of one problem and one conclusion. First, it seems that Deleuze's study of cinema is just as much a study of subjectivity. It would be tempting to say that what he is elaborating is a theory of the subject who enjoys cinema, or views cinema, or creates films. But what I suggested here is that at a very formal level this subject was already described in Deleuze's earlier work. The material subjectivity which experiences cinema's signs is not specifically cinematic. Are the cinema books then a theory of cinema, a theory of subjectivity, or both? I want to leave this question open here.

The conclusion that we *can* draw is that Deleuze's analysis of cinema is clearly a schizoanalysis of cinema. Schizoanalysis was 'a transcendental analysis' – the exploration of a transcendental unconscious. In this sense, *The Logic of Sense* was also an instance of schizoanalysis. It too described a transcendental unconscious beginning with its ultimate elements – partial objects – and traced their evolution through three successive passive syntheses. As long as *Cinema 1* and *Cinema 2* continue this exploration, it is safe to say that they too constitute an example of schizoanalysis.

Chapter 2

Schizoanalysis and the Cinema of the Brain

Gregg Lambert

In his later works, Deleuze referred many times to what he described as
'our new relationship to the Brain'. As he writes in *Cinema 2: The Time-
Image,* because 'the Brain is no more a reasonable system than the world is
rationally constructed [. . .], the brain becomes our illness, our passion,
rather than our mastery, our solution or decision' (Deleuze, 1989: 202). In
other words, there is a crack between the brain and the world; however,
the crack is not 'between', as if the brain was on one side of a vast crevice or
fissure and the world was on the other side, since this would simply redupli-
cate the old Cartesian dualism. Instead, we must now recognize that this
crack is continuous and runs along a plane that stretches between both
terms conceived as purely virtual points; moreover, it is full of hairline
fractures that radiate outward on a plane of immanence that encompasses
both brain and world. What is most remarkable in this remapping of
the earlier divide between objective and subjective conditions of apperception is Deleuze's assertion that the 'interval' between brain and world,
or between stimulus and response, is now governed by a logic of the irrational cut, which is responsible for creating points of uncertainty between
inside and outside (perception or hallucination, associative memory or
reminiscence). Accordingly, the relation between brain and world becomes
a topological point between inside and outside in an uncertain, probabilis-
tic and a-centered system. As Deleuze argues in *Cinema 2,* and later in *What
is Philosophy?* (with Guattari), it is this character of uncertainty that governs
our new relationship to the brain.

Psychoanalysis also proposed the idea of consciousness as an a-centered
and uncertain system by asking the question whether it is 'I' who thinks,
perceives, wills, desires or rather an 'Other' who thinks in my place. But as
Deleuze argues psychoanalysis is based on a rational cerebral model, that of
a semiotic structure or *language*; consequently, the relationship between

brain and world still appears to be 'ordered' according to certain laws or principles that can be mapped onto Euclidean space. It is a structuralist image of the brain that is deterministic and based on the idea of an absolute causality, even when this is assigned to an unconscious level of the psychic apparatus. Even in Lacan, the relationships between signifier and signified, although open to definite metonymic displacements, only appear irrational until they are 'interpreted' by the law of the algorithm, that is, the bar that separates and unifies both series, and which allows for infinite substitutability in the signifying chain. Here, we might understand the algorithmic bar that separates signifier and signified as an image of 'the interval' (*écart*) between inside and outside, which still functions according to a certain model whereby irrational significations can still make sense (thus, the image of the dream-work). This is the importance of understanding that unconscious associations are merely latent semiotic acts that can be reconstructed by analysis and shown to belong to a structure, since 'the Unconscious is structured like a language.' In place of the linguistic model of the Unconscious whose origins are found in Levi-Strauss (here, we must remember the famous statement that the Unconscious is not reservoir for contents any more than the stomach has any relation to the food it digests, but is reduced to a purely symbolic function), or even the later conception of the Unconscious in Lacan, which still operates according to the linguistic principles of metaphor (condensation) and metonymy (displacement), following the work of Gilbert Simondon; Deleuze proposes a new schema that is both non-linguistic (i.e. non-structuralist) and a-centered: that of the 'relative *distribution* of organic internal and external environments (*milieux*)' on a plane that represents an absolute interiority and exteriority, that is, a topological structure of the brain that 'cannot be adequately represented in a Euclidean way' (Deleuze, 1989: 318n31). Instead, Deleuze refers to another cerebral model that is evolving in new studies of the brain by modern sciences, one that is no longer based on a semiotic model, or structural paradigm derived from an earlier metaphysical image of reason. As he writes:

> The discovery of the synapses was enough in itself to shatter the idea of a continuous cerebral system [i.e., the Brain as a whole, or as a unified system], since it laid down irreducible points or cuts . . . [But] in the case of chemical synapses, the point is 'irrational'; the cut is important in itself and belongs to neither of the two sets it separates. . . . 'Hence the greater importance of a factor of uncertainty, or half uncertainty, in the neuronal transmission.' (Deleuze, 1989: 318n32)

Here we see the image of a different algorithmic function than that of the bar separating the two signifying series, but in a certain sense belonging to both as their implicit relation. Instead, we have the image of an 'irrational cut' that operates according to a principle of uncertainty, which implies an entirely different cerebral model, one no longer based on the idea of a deep structure.

This partly explains Deleuze's later interest in modern cinema, which he argues opens to a different manner of depicting thought (or the cerebral interval) no longer based on the semiotic system of language, but rather operates according to the uncertainty principle that governs our relationship to conscious perception. Of course, cinema has always been conceived as a supplemental perception-consciousness apparatus built on the scaffolding of the faculties of perception and the imagination, but how would we revise this secondary or supplemental function when viewed from the perspective of the brain itself? For Deleuze, this is the importance of Eisenstein, who constantly challenged the growing dominance of linguistic formalism for understanding the purely visual logic of cinema. In a certain sense, Deleuze takes up Eisenstein's classic cause against the 'talking cinema' and attempts to develop a new model for understanding the assemblage of optical and sonorous signs in film language (which also includes what Deleuze defines as 'lectosigns', 'chronosigns' and 'noosigns' within a new logic of montage) (Deleuze, 1989: 250–1). Moreover, it is also here that Kubrick becomes an important figure, in some ways complementary to Eisenstein during the period of classical pre-war cinema, since Deleuze argues that all of Kubrick's films function as a *mise en scène* of the brain. On one level, this *mise en scène* can be understood as the depiction of the brain-world organized according to a rational model of which Deleuze recounts many examples in *Cinema 2*: the alignment of the trenches in *Paths of Glory*, the apparatus of Strategic Air Command (SAC) and the military machine or chain of command in *Dr. Strangelove*, the regimented barracks or prison in *Clockwork Orange* and *Full Metal Jacket*, the spaceship *Odyssey* in *2001*, the symmetrical carpet patterns in the hallways of the Hotel Overlook in *The Shining*. On a second level, however, there is an alternative image of the brain that is always depicted as the point of an irrational cut that enters into combat with this first image of the brain and threatens to overturn its order, producing disturbances of association, hallucination, memory and even wild disturbances that are sometimes interpreted through the psychoanalytic conventions of schizophrenia and paranoia. For example, in *Dr. Strangelove* we have the demented mind of General D. Jack Tripper who functions as the expression of an irreducible cerebral crash in the military brain (or the chain of command of SAC), whose dementia could not be, and is ultimately responsible for destroying the world in a nuclear holocaust. Here, Kubrick presents precisely the improbable synapse or connection (communist conspiracy = attack of precious bodily fluids, producing the signifiers O. P. E. and P. O. E.) that functions as the 'irrational cut' causing the whole system to crash. (Of course, the most commonly discussed example of this irrational point is the 'paranoid episode' suffered by Hal 9000 in *2001*.)

In *The Shining*, the 'irrational cut' is represented by the demented mind of the caretaker of the Overlook Hotel, but it is also reflected in the hallucinatory visions of his gifted child Danny (whose gift, moreover, is the result of physical abuse producing both a consequent clairvoyant state and the creation of a double, 'Tony', as a defence against death). It is from both perspectives that the representation of real events that take place opens to both disturbances of memory and perception; in the end, it is the Overlook Hotel itself that represents the dominant point of view (the name itself meaning 'survey', 'spell', even 'trance' or 'hallucination'), the *mise en scène* of a traumatized brain and a psychotic interiority overdetermined by all the events of violence that have taken place in its own history. Thus, for our purposes, *The Shining* represents the most perfect depiction of this new topology of an a-centered cerebral image in which the position of reality cannot be resolved, topologically speaking, either by referring to some external point of view or to a subjectively determined principle of internal projection. Jack's perceptions are, at once, imaginary and real. They are the internal associations of memory belonging to the Hotel and, at the same time, external perceptions of actual events and characters. This uncertainty represents a discontinuous image of the brain, and it is precisely for this reason that the system becomes a-centered, since the interval between stimulus and response, perception and hallucination, can no longer be mapped on the coordinates of external space or interior subjectivity, for these were simply the earlier coordinates used to orient perception-consciousness and thought to a point of objective certainty. This is reinforced by Kubrick's frequent use of doubles in which reality itself is constituted by two identical series (Danny and Tony, the twin girls, symmetrical decorations in the two lounges) that are related by an irrational cut by which they are split apart and joined together again at one point; for example, Danny's finger, or the joined hands of the twins who appear to Danny on the hallway, or the point of identification between Jack and the previous caretaker as actually the same person ('You have always been the caretaker, Mr. Torrance,' says Lloyd, the barkeep). This point, in which the two series are joined together, can be described as a new algorithm of the synaptic function that produces reality through a crease, or fold, in the fabric of the mind itself, representing equally the possibility of both connection and disassociation between brain and world. In fact, Kubrick once commented that in all his films he was drawn precisely to the mechanisms of the uncanny and the double in order to reduce the exercise of reason in providing a measure of defence against the experience of uncertainty, since he argues that it is precisely through the experience of uncertainty that the subject is most closely related to the reality of its own perceptions, memories, thoughts and desires.

At this point, we could return to Descartes and show how revolutionary the situation of an a-centered cerebral system is, in which 'doubt' can no longer function as a method for orienting the distinction between perception and consciousness, but I will reserve this reading for another occasion. I wish to turn instead to demonstrate how the situation described above with regard to the character of uncertainty that governs our new relationship to the brain directly also corresponds to one of the conditions of schizoanalysis as Deleuze and Guattari define it, especially with regard to what they prescribe as the negative or critical task of schizoanalysis, the overturning of the psychoanalytic interpretation of desire, in which modern cinema will have a very special role to play. Thus, in the 'Introduction to Schizoanalysis' (the final section of *Anti-Oedipus*) in response to the question 'How does delirium begin?' they already give us a hint concerning the special relationship between schizoanalysis and cinema when they write: 'Perhaps the cinema is able to capture the movement of madness, precisely because it is not analytical and regressive [as in the case of psychoanalytic interpretation], but explores a global field of co-existence' (Deleuze and Guattari, 2004: 302). But here we must ask: how is it that psychoanalytic interpretation is too analytic and regressive to capture 'the real movement of madness' and how is cinema able to explore 'a global field of co-existence' to reveal the true conditions of delirium? Already implicit in Deleuze and Guattari's question is the presumption that what they call 'delirium' will become the special province for schizoanalysis, but this is no less true for the psychoanalytic interpretation of unconscious desire, for as they write elsewhere 'desire is delirium'; or rather, 'delirium is the general matrix of every unconscious social investment' (Deleuze and Guattari, 2004: 305).

Let us take the classical Oedipal scenario. Here, desire is represented as a paranoid idea that first appears in the mind of the father, which then is projected into the position of the child as the internalized feeling of guilt.

Thus, 'the paranoiac father Oedipalizes the son,' and it is the error specific to the psychoanalytic interpretation of desire to act as if things begin with the child. The problem of this reversal and this displacement of the real conditions of desire is that it is already presented as an internalized projection of the father that is experienced in the position of the son, and this produces its infinitely regressive character: 'the father must have been a child, but was able to be a child only in relation to a father, who was himself a child, in relation to another father,' and so on, all the way to the position an absolutely primary father who can only be posited in the cyclical form of myth (i.e. the primal position of the father of the horde). What is missed altogether is the reality of desire itself experienced by both the son and the father simultaneously, since both are 'plunged' into the social field from which the specific investment of desire first emerges as a paranoid idea, on the part of the father, or as an internalized feeling of guilt, on the part of the son. Both the father and the son, assuming that they are not the same individual, or share the same demented brain that has undergone both condensation and displacement, experience a common delirium whose first instance is to be found in the social field, which breaks the infinite regress of desire by locating its real conditions outside the family. Hence, as Deleuze and Guattari write, 'the father is first in relation to the child, but only because what is first is the social investment in relation to the familial investment, the investment of the social field in which the father, the child, and the family as a sub-aggregate are at once and the same time immersed' (Deleuze and Guattari, 2004: 305–6).

How would then cinema be capable of revealing the co-existence of these two fields without resorting to another regressive hypothesis? Here, again, Kubrick's portrayal of both the objective and subjective conditions of madness or delirium appears exemplary. As we have already see in the previous examples, Kubrick uses the outbreak of delirium as a topological location to map the subject's relation directly to the social assemblage in which it belongs: General Ripper's madness and command and control apparatus of the Strategic Air Command, Jack's murderous rage and the social field constituted by the Overlook Hotel invested with all the excesses of class desire; in *Clockwork Orange*, criminal delinquency and the prison assemblage or that of the cinematic assemblage itself fuelled by sex and violence, or Pyle's psychotic breakdown and that of the military-barracks assemblage in *Full Metal Jacket;* finally, even Hal 9000's so-called 'paranoid break' must be understood as co-extensive with the paranoid delirium of the scientific-technological assemblage that seeks to penetrate the monolith in order to reveal the intentionality of the alien brain that created it, a desire that is clearly shown to emerge at the beginning of human history with the discovery of weaponry as a means to subjugate the environment in order to get a good night's sleep. In each case, Kubrick shows that subjective delirium is co-extensive within the social field that invests it with reality.

As my primary example of this, I wish to turn to Kubrick's initial conception of *A.I.*, the film later realized by Steven Spielberg, in order to demonstrate the possibility of employing certain cinematic narratives – certainly, not all! – to explore the social field constituted by delirium-desire. In this case, the specific delirium in question is 'love', or rather, 'Mommy-love' (the social delirium that consolidates the subjective relations that compose the Oedipal family). As Kubrick once said concerning the idea of love, 'It's not going to be easy to circumvent our primitive emotional programming,' and so here I am only speculating that Kubrick's version would have given us a more realistic exploration of this primitive social idea (cited in Phillips, 2001: 67). In fact, it is this question that Kubrick is most interested in exploring: the question of whether human love is merely the result of our 'primitive emotional programming', which is to say our semi-autonomous desiring-machines, and how to account for the cerebral function of love as an 'irrational cut', that is, for the determination of the particular objects or subjects that we choose to love without resorting to the notion of a Structure, that is, to Oedipus? However, in order to demonstrate how Kubrick might have resolved this dilemma, it will be necessary to pry open the obverse underside of Spielberg's Oedipalized version.

First, let us go back to the primal scene where boy-robot's love program is activated to create the passionate attachment to Mommy. Here, Mommy turns on a switch in David's head and repeats a string of signifiers that have no meaning other than they are said in a signifying chain that must be exact and that they be uttered while looking into the boy's eyes. This turns on the boy's love program, so to speak, or turns the relation Monica-David into Mommy-me, a relation that henceforth is not open to substitution or further combination. The fact that this 'order' functions as the reverse of the normal installation of the Symbolic is crucial, since Oedipus functions precisely by setting up the possibility of symbolic substitution or the metonymic displacement of the original signified under the bar of the signifier. Therefore, here we have located the cause for the failure or break-down of David's love program, since it institutes what psychoanalysis would define as regression, that is, a fixation on the primitive terms of signifying relation, a refusal of opening this relation to symbolic exchange or substitution that is usually identified in the borderline subjects of psychosis or schizophrenia.

However, turning back to the actual film, things begin to go awry
only with the return of Martin who, according to a traditional psychoanalytic would merely represent the desire of the Father (who seems strangely
distant in Spielberg's version, but who plays a crucial role in sending David
off into exile). At this point, suffering a certain estrangement from Mommy,
David assumes (along with Teddy) the position of a cast-away toy at the foot
of Martin's bed where he listens with wonderment as Mommy reads from
the book of his desire, according to which the narrative of Pinocchio will
suddenly represent the 'irrational cut' that sets a mechanical boy to go off
in search of the Blue Fairy who will transform him into a real boy – because
'mommy only loves real boys'. However, this narrative only functions as a
screen or the metaphoric condensation of another narrative in which
a man goes to the end of the world, beyond the finite borders of time
and death itself, in order to fulfil the fantasy of one day waking up in the
bed of his beloved. Thus, the Oedipal trauma introduced by the statement
'Mommy only loves real boys' must actually be heard at the same time as
another series where 'Monica only loves real men'. It is at this point that
the narrative is the most literal or realistic portrayals of masculine desire,
since under the regime of Oedipus all males must become estranged from
their original passionate attachment and set off in search of a blue fairy
who, with a wave of her magic wand, will turn them into real men. If we strip
away the function of metaphor, what Spielberg provides is a narrative of
romantic love, which is merely the repressed convention that structures the
idealized narrative of Oedipal sexuality itself.

In order to account for this uncanny effect of the co-implication of one
narrative within another, it is not just that Spielberg did not see the unconscious resonance, or identity, between these two narratives that I imagine
interested Kubrick with the script originally, and thus failed to make it
function as a double, since Spielberg is not responsible for creating these
narratives, but only for arranging their relationship in such a way that both
can be co-present to determine the idea of love only under the condition
that one remains repressed, in such a way that any overt identification of
their literal meaning is submitted to the law of metaphor (i.e. to repression
proper). The question becomes what is the source of this repression, and
we do not have to search far in order to see that the field of culture (i.e.
Language itself) is replete with myths and fabulous tales about love that
Lacan once compared to the explanation of an old woman concerning the
mysteries of Daphne and Cloe – all of which function to protect the subject
from ever encountering the reality of desire. After all, how do we learn to
desire except by means of rumours and hearsay? The fact that Spielberg

chooses Pinocchio for his explanation only reveals that he is just as igno-rant as the rest of us on this question, and it is by the special gift of his ignorance that he has become a great popular storyteller since he chooses stories full of unconscious resonances that are allowed to be enjoyed pre-cisely because they are repressed.

It is precisely here that I see the special function of modern cinema for exploring unconscious investments in the social field. Film is 'a body' since it sees, it feels and it even speaks. The fact that cinematic 'feelings' are no less constituted by conventions and clichés, the little habits of sensa-tion, make it almost equivalent to the natural body constituted by habit and by instinct. For example, how is the feeling of love expressed? Here we have the tradition of a limited number of forms combined with little scenes and sound images: the sound of the ocean, the close up of the face, soft music. It is not very different from the different combinations possible for the expression of love in so-called real life, and even constitutes a reflec-tion on its completely artificial or traditional semiotics. Love is expressed by a series of clichés which the subject chooses to invest with singularity; however, singularity is only made possible because of the linguistic regime of the cliché, the fact that its finite expression is so over-determined by rep-etition that it reaches a point of meaninglessness, and for this reason it is capable of expressing a pure intensity. The statement 'I love you' can only make sense to one by the very fact that it is a universal statement. It is non-sense, but because it is non-sense, it is capable of expressing the real of the subject's 'I feel'. The statement makes sense as a linguistic unit because it excludes meaning on a linguistic level in order to include it as a pure affect of the statement itself. It is purely performative and, in this sense, it belongs to the same category as the statements 'I understand', and 'I see', both statements that refer to nothing beyond the performance of the state they signal. Because the statement refers to a pure intensity, however, or is itself representative of an intensive state, its meaning can only be measured on an a-semiotic level of the utterance.

Film deals with tradition as well, and there is a social significance that also determines its conventions for producing meaningful depictions of the subject's 'I Feel'. What distinguishes the former is the social assem-blage that restricts its possibility and makes it scarce, so to speak. For example, the statement 'I love you' between mother and child should not combine the affect ('I feel') in romantic expression; this association is possible, but must be repressed as an overt or consciousness meaning. Social convention exists to repress such a performative sense in such an occasion; however, its possibility still exists as an attribute of the statement,

which can be realized in certain special circumstances or perverse scenarios. Thus, we have the universal myth of Oedipus, of which only Freud
perceived the supreme irony that, in fact, this is not a myth at all, but
rather a literal truth: all children (all male children) must be exiled from
the original familial unit only to return to it as a stranger and occupy the
original position of the father, which is to say he must supplant to father's
position in fucking his mother. This is literally the truth, which is to say
it is structurally necessary for the perpetuation of the family as a social institution. It could not be otherwise. But it is here where we must locate the
mythic structure, since *mythos* in the Greek names a certain technique of
narrative which is open to substitution, allegory and symbol; this is because
myths are narratives of what remains beyond conscious life of the individuals, but tell of things that are either before or after the individual
consciousness. Thus, in order to guarantee its perpetuation as a structure,
for the family as a social institution to survive catastrophe, it must strategi-
cally build into its structural reproduction those occasions of substitution,
mistaken identity, misrecognition and unconsciousness as absolutely essential to its perpetuation. It is here precisely we find the concept of modern
love as a convention stocked full of clichés, signs and symbols.

It is precisely at this point, according to the psychoanalytic myth of
Oedipus, that the Family as a social institution and Language as a human
institution are inextricably involved in a plot, a vast conspiracy, to trick the
individual; the possibilities of metaphor (condensation) and displacement
(metonymy) are provided to the family to serve its aim in reproducing
its own identity. Thus, Oedipus returns to Thebes as a stranger and mistak-
enly murders his father and unknowingly sleeps with his mother. Or the
child is a stranger who unconsciously replaces his father in assuming a
role with a displaced representative of the mother. Here, the qualities of
anonymity (strangeness), disguise, displacement and a certain arbitrary
symbolism of terms in relation to their original representatives are the functions of the unconscious structure of Desire. For Freud, Oedipus is true
and not the anomaly that is presented by Sophocles. The only anomaly that
Freud perceived was the expression of the structure itself: that given the
family is only able to perpetuate itself through disguise and displacement of
its elements, it is structurally possible the elements that belong to the same
structure might be mistaken for their original terms and thus lead the entire
structure into contradiction, threatening the structure itself with non-
sense. Because 'incest' constituted the very transcendental border of the
social form for Freud, this is the crisis that the Oedipus complex represents
for Freud, so that neurosis must function as a 'stop-gap' to prevent the

identification with the original terms from ever being realized. Sophocles' Oedipus, after all, is a social drama based on what happens to the family if this should ever occur – absolute destitution and the suicide of all its members.

What is this limit to the symbolic series of substitutions that Freud always held as the limit represented by the prohibition of incest? Is incest itself a limit in a transcendental sense, or is it simply the prohibited barrier of non-sense introduced by the structure which makes it both absolutely necessary for the structure to function, and for this reason unthinkable in its own terms. It is, as Lacan would say, precisely where we do not think to think. Incest would refer to the position of the nonhuman sex in sex, to the machinic dimension of sex, to structure itself. If it functions as a limit, it is only in the sense that it refers to another organization of desire that cannot be included as variations already made possible by the structural arrangements, as either their possible displacement within a series, or disguise of one series by another, but would open to an entirely different organization, which Deleuze calls 'nonhuman sex'. Concerning this nonhuman sex, Deleuze comments:

> In a difficult and beautiful [text], Marx called for the necessity to think human sexuality not only as a relation between the human sexes, masculine and feminine, but as a relation between 'human sex and nonhuman sex.' He was clearly not thinking of animals, but what is nonhuman in human sexuality: the machines of desire. (Deleuze, 2004: 243)

In this passage, it is crucial to observe that Deleuze derives this 'nonhuman sex' not from Freud, but rather from Marx, where the nonhuman sex refers to the machine, to the machinery of production that determines the possibility of Desire as a function that belongs to a social assemblage. What if the nonhuman sex in human sex is the structure of sexuality itself?

In conclusion, therefore, I would propose that the possible schizoanalysis of love would treat what Deleuze called the 'nonhuman sex' in human sexuality, where Desire would not speak, would not have anything to say to us, not even in the deepest point of our dreams and our fantasies, where, under a psychoanalytic interpretation of the Unconscious, desire never stops speaking of its own possibility (as well as of its prohibited possibilities as well) as already determined by the laws of the signifying regime laid down by a certain image of Structure. The object of a schizoanalysis of love as a social form would be the underlying unconscious investments that belong to our collective fantasies, and if I have analysed *A.I.* as a horror story, according to the conventions of an Oedipal economy, it is only to prove the point that Oedipus is still walking and shaking his chains through the hallways of our social existence.

The goals of schizoanaylsis are two-fold: to critique the machinery by which the Unconscious is produced today under the regime of Oedipal economy, which Deleuze and Guattari define as the negative or critical goal that must always accompany a positive affirmation of Desire as innocent, in some sense, to the trappings of this economy. Although I have not high-lighted this positive or affirmative dimension in my reading of Kubrick, I think at least I have laid out the direction that this affirmation would explore: de-personalize the unconscious and liberate fantasy from its structure! As Deleuze says, it is 'as if desire had nothing to say, but rather was the assemblage of tiny machines, desiring machines, always in a particu-lar relation to big social machines and the technological machines' (Deleuze, 2004: 243).

Therefore, 'what are your particular desiring machines?' This would be the first question of any schizoanalysis. It is here also, I believe, that there is a special province for cinema today, which itself is made up of the assem-blage of signs and particular conventions, which are the machines for producing love, for giving love meaning today, in the sense of constantly reanimating a dead corpse in order that it can emulate again the Spirit that governs our social lives. Deleuze's own battle-cry was to liberate the brain from the dominance of a too-structured brain, which is to say from all ready-made linkages, myths and clichés; in other words, to break out of the same compulsory structures and narrative linkages, the same dreary stories, the same desires and same horrors as only Oedipus can dream. It is here, in the positive task that Deleuze assigns to a future cinema (one that as of yet does not exist, or only exists virtually in films that are rarely realized), that the combinatory art of the narrative of images and sounds is directly con-nected to the positive creation of a new image of the brain.

Chapter 3

Losing Face

Gregory Flaxman and Elena Oxman

Lose your face. Become capable of loving without remembering, without phantasm and without interpretation, without taking stock. Let there just be fluxes, which sometimes dry up, freeze or overflow, which sometimes combine or diverge.
                                                                    —*Gilles Deleuze*, Dialogues

About face

In his own writings, and especially in his writings with Félix Guattari, Gilles Deleuze makes the face one of the most integral concepts, recurrent figures and fundamental problems of philosophy. The face is ubiquitous, appearing (among so many other places) in *Difference and Repetition* as a key component of the Other Person; in *Mille Plateaus* as the white wall/black hole surface of faciality (*visageité*); in *Cinema 1* as the affection-image; and again, in *What Is Philosophy?*, as the face of the Other Person. Far from remaining consistent across these terrains, the face undergoes a series of variations – or, better yet, the variations of the face constitute a series – whose logic remains at once indisputably important and invariably vague. What is the relation between these different faces of the face and, ultimately, how do they function in Deleuze and Guattari's work? In their philosophy, which they define as 'constructivism', the authors always relate thinking to the posing of problems, but what kind of problem is the face? It strikes us that, across the range of its manifestations, the face is not simply the site of a recurring problem but, rather, that *the face renders thinking problematic*.

For Deleuze and Guattari, thinking only begins at the point when it stops simply providing solutions and, instead, accedes to the paradoxical form of a problematism. The problem as such constitutes an impower (*impouvoir*), a kind of blockage that stops thinking in its tracks, but this affective paralysis is no less the moment that we are compelled to undertake 'what is called thinking' (Heidegger). Thinking always demands a kind of provocation, or even violence, which compels us to stray from the automatism of our habits, clichés and opinions. Hence, when Deleuze and Guattari say that 'something in the world forces us to think,' they mean that even the kind of thought we call philosophy only exists in relation to a 'non-philosophical' domain, or a 'no', to which philosophy responds and from which it extracts its own (*propre*) problem, even the problem of thought itself (Deleuze, 1994: 139). Ultimately, then, the essay to follow concerns the complex dynamism which thinking catalyses in Deleuze and Guattari's work between philosophy and non-philosophy, bearing us from the plane of their conceptual constructivism to the sphere of cinematic images to the practice of schizoanalysis. In each of these domains, we might say, the problem of thinking is staged through the face – first conceptually (as the 'Other Person'), then imagistically (as the 'affect-image'), and finally politically (as 'faciality').

Above all else, this essay contends that the face itself forms a critical region of non-philosophy: even as their renderings and descriptions of the face draw from recognizable sources, there remains the sense that Deleuze and Guattari find in the face the potential to encounter something essentially unrecognizable. We might call this the schizoanalytic potential of the face – a potential for its *effacement*, where singularities of expression are detached from their subjective coordinates, and we discover the anonymity of an affection that is at once an image of feeling-thinking and an image demanding to be thought. In particular, it is in the domain of the cinema that we discover the conditions necessary for the effacement of the face – for a line of flight 'toward the regions of the asignifying, the asubjective and the faceless' (Deleuze and Guattari, 1987: 187). When it is no longer considered as the locus of subjectivity, nor of contemplation nor even of perception, the face becomes the non-place of an encounter between the subject and an asubjective becoming, between faciality and its effacement, between thinking and an unthought.

Facing the Other Person

When philosophy claims a genesis or beginning, and 'it is not obvious that it must', as Deleuze and Guattari note, this does not imply a fixed point of origin but an originating power of conceptualization in response to a problem (Deleuze and Guattari, 1994: 15). 'All concepts are connected to problems,' they explain, 'without which they would have no meaning and which can themselves only be isolated or understood as their solution emerges'. Only in relation to problems do concepts discover a certain 'point of view or ground [*raison*]' which they address and with which they combine (1994: 16). It is in this light that we might consider what Deleuze and Guattari call the 'Other Person' as the first concept of philosophy – provided that we approach this apriority with all due irony, rendering it first only in relation to a non-philosophy that precludes any such enumeration.[1] In this sense, the Other Person designates one place, among countless other, from which to begin thinking, but it is nonetheless the place at which we can pose thinking as a problem. Deleuze and Guattari phrase the problem as follows: 'is another person [*autrui*] necessarily second in relation to a self?' (1994: 16). If the self is first and the other second, we may say that the other is a subject that presents itself as an object in relation to a self (to 'me'). Yet we might just as readily identify the Other Person with another subject, for whom 'I' now appear as a special object; now, 'it is me who is the Other Person as I appear to that subject' (Deleuze and Guattari, 1994: 16).[2]

When we pose the question of the Other Person this way, asking whether it is 'first' or 'second', we immediately invoke the problem in terms that, while giving rise to other concepts (special object, subject, self), reduces them all to a matter of priority: which came first or, even more to the point, which caused which? Are we dealing with an *a priori* Other or an *a priori* self? This field of indeterminacy already suggests the contours of another problem, which emerges by recasting the first one: what if instead of asking which comes first, self or other person, we inquire into the nature of the *positions* that define self and Other Person, or even subject and object? Better yet, what are the relations that determine the variability of the Other Person and its components – components that can be concepts in their own right? Posing the problem in this way, the Other Person designates neither a special object, not an other subject, nor a self, but the position that all three may occupy. If the Other Person requires a different concept, no less a concept of difference, this is because the problem of the Other Person concerns 'the plurality of subjects, their relationship, and their reciprocal presentation' (Deleuze and Guattari, 1994: 16). In other words, the concept here immediately produces several subjects.

Therefore, when Deleuze and Guattari ask, 'On what conditions is a concept first, not absolutely but in relation to another?' we should already intuit that the 'first' here does not indicate an origin but the origination of a variability at the heart of conceptual creation – the variability of relations which the concept organizes and from which the concept is inseparable.

The emergence of the Other Person as a concept, its moment of construction, is also a 'heterogenesis' insofar as it carries out an 'ordering' of qualitatively 'different components' (Deleuze and Guattari, 1994: 20). Thus, when Deleuze and Guattari construct the Other Person, they incarnate an 'image of thought' that, in turn, unleashes its distributing power across a conceptual landscape:

> There is at some moment a calm and restful world. Suddenly a frightened face looms up that looks at something out of the field. The Other Person appears here as neither subject nor object but as something that is very different: a possible world, the possibility of a frightening world. This possible world is not real, or not yet, but it exists nonetheless: it is an expressed that exists only in its expression – the face or an equivalent of the face. (1994: 17)

What is the nature of this conceptual terrain, no less the 'image of thought' which organizes it? First, we must note that we are no longer situated in the position of either subject or object, depending on the point of view; rather, we are confronted with an indeterminate landscape (a 'there is . . .') in the midst of which the anonymous face which suddenly appears is neither self nor other – it is not anyone, or literally a 'no one', or an indeterminate 'one' which exists only as the possibility of a 'frightening' world. Rather than subjects, objects, selves and others, we begin with the face and the possible world, to which a third element may yet be added – the language or speech that gives reality to the possible when it is 'spoken about in a given field of experience' (Deleuze and Guattari, 1994: 18). The Other Person is the 'point of condensation' for these 'three inseparable components: possible world, existing face and real language or speech' (Deleuze and Guattari, 1994: 18).

We are now in a position to understand why the Other Person serves as a kind of first concept for Deleuze and Guattari – not because it is 'first' in an absolute sense but because it communicates the variable relations according to which philosophy begins. The Other Person does not concern the particularity of any subject because its concept (no less the concepts of the subject, the object and the self) takes shape according to an assemblage of relations – and as Deleuze and Guattari remind us, *relations are never internal to their terms*. In orienting the distribution of relations, the Other Person makes thinking an infinitely supple modulation of conditions in response to a perceptual field: 'no longer being either the subject of the field or the object in the field, the Other Person will become the condition under which not only subject and object are redistributed but also figure and ground, margins and center, moving object and reference point, transitive and subjective, length and depth' (1994: 18). In this respect, notably, the formulation of the Other Person can be understood as a remarkable revision of Kant's 'transcendental aesthetic'. If the latter continues to depend upon the subject qua categories as the conditions of possible experience, Deleuze and Guattari make the Other Person the condition of not only the subject but also of 'perception, for ourselves and for others' (1994: 18). This is no easy distinction, relying as it does on the transformation of what Kant calls the 'subjective constitution of our mind' (Kant, 1965: 68) into an organization or combination of components which are neither interior nor exterior but which, instead, distribute the series of intensity and extensity.

In the Kantian and neo-Kantian tradition, the conditions of possibility prototypically precede, determine and delimit experience in advance of experience, effectively rendering the real in accordance with the legislation of what 'can be' felt, perceived or thought. But as Deleuze writes: 'It is strange that aesthetics (as the science of the sensible) could be founded on what *can* be represented in the sensible,' for the regime of representation consigns philosophy to ignoring the 'reality of the real insofar as it is thought' (Deleuze, 1994: 56). It is in this vein that Deleuze and Guattari evoke the Other Person in order to displace experience from the sphere of transcendental idealism, which determines its possibilities within already given parameters, into a transcendental (or superior) empiricism. As early as *Diffference and Repetition*, Deleuze declares that 'we are surrounded by possibles, but our possibles are always others' (1994: 260). In other words, the real is not conditioned by virtue of prior possibles; rather, the real gives rise to possible worlds that surround us but have not been actualized. Rather than begin from the perspective of conditions of *possible* experience, then, we turn to the Other Person – or, rather, the Other Person turns to us, confronts us with its singular expression of fear and, thence, presents the face of a possible world as a condition of *real* experience – an 'intrinsic genesis, not an extrinsic conditioning' (Deleuze, 1994: 154).We are not saying that experience is 'all there is', as if with the absence of idealism we lapse into chaotic flux of experience; rather, experience itself forms the stipulations according to which the possible will be understood, and the possible is absolutely real even though it resembles nothing: the face does not resemble what terrifies it. We should say that the possible, rather than existing, insists: it is there, implicated and enveloped in the expression of the Other Person.

Framing the face

Whence the special importance of the face, which functions as a component of the concept of the Other Person but to which we must turn as a concept and a problem in its own right. Consider once more the frightened face of the Other Person: even though the source of its fear remains unseen, the face nevertheless expresses fear or, rather, produces that fear, no less the suspicion of its cause. We are simultaneously in the presence of a real image of expression and a possible world which remains out of field (*hors champs*), but as Deleuze and Guattari insist, the possible is no less real because it is sensed and sensible, imprinted upon a face as that which is felt and expressed. It is no wonder, then, that Deleuze and Guattari develop the problematic of the face in the domains of cinema and schizoanalysis, since the face is both an expression of the possible as such and the surface on which determinations will be mapped, an implicating force of expression and its looming signification – its explication as something *else*. We might even say that cinema and schizoanalysis define two axes of the (Janus) face's problematic, ranging as it does from the expression of thinking (the affection-image) to the politics of thought (faciality).

For our purposes, we begin with the cinema, since it provides a unique means to think about the Other Person in general and the face in particular. We know that Deleuze always avowed that 'certain philosophical problems pushed me to seek out the solutions in cinema', but this is particularly the case with the problem of the face (Deleuze, 2006: 285). Take the description of the Other Person on which Deleuze and Guattari place such emphasis: 'There is at some moment a calm and restful world. Suddenly a frightened face looms up . . .' (1994: 17). The concept of the Other Person here takes shape according to a kind of occasion or scenario. The concept configures its components (empty field, looming face, possible world) according to a kind of *mise-en-scene*, and it is this manner of performing the concept, which is inseparable from the concept itself, on which we might linger. Above all else, we should grasp the Other Person according to its framing (*cadrage*). The scene is set, the drama or dynamism established, by virtue of an image of space, as if a camera had been placed in the midst of an incomprehensible landscape: we find no structures, no points of reference, only a stray rectangle of space – let us say, a desert – into which, without warning, 'a frightened face looms up that looks at something out of field'. The frame is suddenly filled by the image of the Other Person who seems to provide an anchoring point for what we see. The face of the Other captures the frame, but it is also captivated by that which is 'out of frame' (*hors cadre*). It is in this sense that the face described by Deleuze and Guattari always faces two sides, distributing both that which we see, its own features, and that which it sees, which will play across those features. The face that 'looms up' in the frame, gathering its features in a constellation of fright, equally constitutes an image in relation to an off-screen – in relation to a frightening world which the face, in turn, *expresses*.

Thus, in *Cinema 1* Deleuze defines the face as a close-up or *affection-image*, which is to say, 'a power or quality considered for itself, as expressed' (Deleuze, 2001: 97). In this sense, the analysis of affection that Deleuze undertakes, both with and without Guattari, is anchored to draws from Henri Bergson, who provides the most basic definition of the term. Affection 'is a motor tendency on a sensitive nerve' (Deleuze, 2001: 87), but the face is the locus of affection and the image of its sensation (Deleuze, 1986: 5). The face is subject to emotions and intensities that, given what Deleuze calls its 'relative immobility and its receptive organs', it can do no better than wear on its face (Deleuze, 2001: 66). Because it is virtually powerless, the face claims the capacity to incarnate a virtual image of power – the power to be affected, to 'bring to light movements of expression while they remain frequently buried in the rest of the body' (Deleuze, 2001: 66). A series of micro-movements, or vibrations, pass across the face: gawking eyes, a furrowed brow, perhaps the hint of a gasp . . . fear. The legibility of the face consists in the affections that, passing over this receptive surface, resolve themselves into expressions that just as quickly dissolve themselves into others. While the face is the expressed, the passage of affection plays on its surface as the expression which escapes the solid landscape of features like the smile of the Cheshire cat.

In this light, we should already grasp the importance of the cinema for the analytics of the face, since with the close-up, the medium appropriates a distinct power or capacity to deterritorialize the face, tearing it from a body. Inasmuch as every cinematic image constitutes a kind of deterritorialization, the frame having wrested the image from its larger milieu, Deleuze insists that 'there is a very special kind of deterritorialization which is specific to the affection- image' (Deleuze, 2001: 96). While the perception-image and action-image 'translate' movement into objects of perception or acts of a subject, with the affection-image, a pure quality is called forth: 'It is precisely in affection that the movement ceases to be that of translation in order to become movement of expression, that is to say quality, simple tendency that stirs up an immobile element' (Deleuze, 2001: 66). Because it is neither transformed into the objects of perception nor into the acts of a subject, the affection-image opens up a synapse between perception and action. The translation between received movement and executed movement is short-circuited so that the externalization of affect into a motor-tendency is absorbed and involuted. Therefore, in the cinema as perhaps nowhere else, the face can become a hesitation, an affective intensity that prolongs itself in an expression in relation to something 'as yet' to be seen or a 'not yet' decided. The face designates a zone of implicated intensity, which, rather than extending into action or perception vibrates as a pure quality considered for itself (see Deleuze, 1994: 260). It is in this respect that the 'first concept' of the Other Person is inseparable from the *firstness* of the face. In *Cinema 1*, firstness 'is that which is as it is for itself and in itself . . . It is not a sensation, a feeling, an idea, but the quality of a possible sensation, feeling or idea. Firstness is thus the category of the Possible: it gives a proper consistency to the possible, it expresses the possible without actualizing it, whilst making it a complete mode' (Deleuze, 2001: 98). If the Other Person is the first concept, this is because its affective zone, the face, is the locus of firstness, of 'qualities or powers considered for themselves, without reference to anything else, independently of any question of their actualization' (Deleuze, 2001: 98), and if the Other Person 'begins' philosophy, this is only insofar as its firstness expresses a certain 'impower' of thought, which is also the power of the Possible as such.

Nevertheless, we should recall that the Other Person, as the expression of a possible world, is also actualized as a specific 'person', as an 'I', when it expresses itself in language. 'When the expressing speaks and says, "I am frightened", even if its words are untruthful, this is enough for reality to be given to the possible as such. This is the only meaning of the "I" as linguistic index' (Deleuze and Guattari, 1994: 17). Thus, if the face of the Other implicates the possible world which it expresses, it is also the terrain of an individualizing function which determines it as the face of *someone*. We might say that the face has one side turned towards expression and another towards actualization – a dual existence which is demonstrated nowhere more clearly than in the cinema. According to Deleuze, the faces that we see in cinema are more often than not determined within the sensory-motor schema whereby affection is converted into action. In the cinema, Deleuze argues, the realm of the action-image is the seat of habit and recognition according to which the face acquires a subjective dimension. Thus, as much as the powers or qualities of the face can exist 'for themselves, as expressed', they can also exist 'as actualized, embodied in states of things' (Deleuze, 2001: 97). Indeed, we can juxtapose the pure quality of affection with what happens when the affection-image gives rise to an action-image: 'in a state of things which actualizes them, the quality becomes the quality of an object, power becomes action or passion, affect becomes sensation, sentiment, emotion or even impulse in a person, the face becomes the character or mask of the person' (Deleuze, 2001: 97).

Persona non grata

We can thus begin to understand how the circuit that we have followed, from the concept of the Other Person to the affection-image, finally leads us to Deleuze and Guattari's schizoanalytic project. Specifically, it is in the context of his writing on the affection-image that Deleuze begins to circumscribe the problem to which the modern face gives rise, namely, the determination of subjective, signifying faces. With the action-image, we might say that the face acquires a 'person' to which it belongs, and indeed, Deleuze specifies the three 'personalizing' functions of the face: 'it is individuating (it distinguishes or characterizes each person); it is socializing (it manifests a social role); it is relational or communicating (it ensures not only communication between two people but also, in a single person, the internal agreement between his character and his role)' (Deleuze, 2001: 99). Deleuze and Guattari are concerned with precisely these functions of the face in their schizoanalytic project, where the dangers and possibilities of the face's affective landscape are cashed out as a politics and a practice.

Deleuze and Guattari have always maintained that 'concepts have a history', but in the framework of our discussion to this point, we should understand this in two distinct (albeit related) senses. In the first place, of course, we are in the midst of developing the history of their own concept of the face, which has taken us from philosophy to the cinema and, now, to schizoanalysis. But in the second place, it is in the very context of schizoanalysis that Deleuze and Guattari, having turned to the face as the locus of the Other Person, declare that the face itself has a history. 'If we consider primitive societies', they write, 'we see that there is very little that operates through the face: their semiotic is nonsignifying, nonsubjective, essentially collective, polyvocal, and corporeal, playing on very diverse forms and substances' (Deleuze and Guattari, 1987: 175). Indeed, we could say that the importance that contemporary Western culture attributes to the face would be impossible to imagine outside the emergence of subjectivity as the means of organizing and disciplining thinking itself. Deleuze and Guattari define this organization – or faciality – along the lines of an abstract machine which effectively produces the face (as we know it) in accordance with a particular assemblage of forces. 'It is precisely because the face depends on an abstract machine that it does not presume a pre-existent subject or signifier' (Deleuze and Guattari, 1987: 180): rather, the abstract machine of expression produces the face as a signifying subjectivity or a 'signifying biuni-vocalization and subjective binarization' (Deleuze and Guattari, 1987: 179).

Historically – or, better yet, epistemically – the face is engendered when the abstract machine carries out an 'absolute' deterritorialization of the head from the stratum of the organism to the stratum of the mixed-semiotic. Insofar as it is deterritorialized from the organism, Deleuze and Guattari explain, the face becomes a 'substance of expression' which is reterritorialized onto 'the strata of significance and subjectification' (1987: 181). On the one hand, significance qua signification constitutes an 'elementary face in relation with another: it is a man or a woman, a rich person or a poor one, an adult or a child, a leader or a subject "an x or a y"'. On the other hand, subjectification ensures that even exceptionality is incorporated into its grid ('A ha! It's not a man and it's not a woman, so it must be a transvestite') (1987: 177). For this reason, Deleuze and Guattari never cease to remind us that, even though faces are produced, we do not produce our own faces: 'you don't so much have a face as slide into one' (1987: 177). Far from being individual, faces 'define zones of frequency or probability' for the encoding of redundancies (1987: 168). Faces are subject to a perpetual recoding whereby they are determined within a field of legibility that we are in the process of analysing. Indeed, under-standing the face in these terms – not simply as happy or sad, peaceful or mad, but as the locus of power for these encodings – is no easy task, but we can best glean the reterritorialization of meaning onto this enigmatic surface *('sur-face')* by turning once more to the cinema.

While the cinema may not be the inaugural event of faciality, we have already marked the cinema as the paradigmatic moment and medium of this eventuality. For Deleuze and Guattari, the close-up is tantamount to the abstract machine of faciality, so much so that they will suggest that the face itself is a close-up 'avant le cinema', whereas the literal cinematic close-up, whatever its object (a clock, a knife, a hand), is always facialized. The face is 'by nature a close-up, with its inanimate white surfaces, its shining black holes, its emptiness and boredom' (1987: 171). Inasmuch as the face is implicated in a politics, Deleuze and Guattari seek to develop a politics of the face that would consist in its very dismantling. Needless to say, this politics should not be confused with some kind of humanist nostalgia for a 'time before faces'; it is not 'a question of "returning" to presignifying and presubjective semiotics of primitive peoples' (1987: 188). As Deleuze and Guattari insist, 'there are only inhumanities, humans are made exclusively of inhumanities, but very different ones, of very different natures and speeds'. Indeed, the face is the 'inhuman in human beings', so much so that,

> [I]f human beings have a destiny it is to escape the face, to dismantle the face and facializations, to become imperceptible, to become clandestine, not by returning to animality nor even by returning to the head, but by quite spiritual and special becoming animal, by strange true becomings that get past the wall and get out of the black holes, that make faciality traits themselves finally elude the organization of the face – freckles dashing toward the horizon, hair carried off by the wind, eyes you traverse instead of seeing yourself in or gazing into those glum face to face encounters between signifying subjectivities. (1987: 171)

If the face is caught up in or captured by politics, the politics of the face constitutes a project to dismantle its determinations. Rather than returning to a 'human' face, Deleuze and Guattari augur an entirely different procedure whereby the face could become the site of a becoming-imperceptible, extending a line of flight 'toward the regions of the asignifying, the asubjective and the faceless' (1987: 187).

Preceding his work with Guattari, Deleuze had stressed that the basis of both a creative philosophy and creative politics ought to be sought in 'special conditions of experience, however artificial', when the face, far from being determined, once more opens up possible worlds (Deleuze, 1994: 260). In the context of schizoanalysis, however, these 'artificial' conditions are in some sense spelt out, for as Deleuze and Guattari write, it 'requires all the resources of art' to escape the face (1987: 187). We have seen how the close-up can produce an abstract machine of facility such that the face becomes the character or mask of the person (Deleuze, 2001: 97), but now we have reached a point where we can grasp the medium's even more radical power. In as much as the affection-image enjoys a special relationship to the face, abstracting it from determinate milieus and expressing its affective singularities in unprecedented durations, it enjoys the occasional power to go through the face – to tear the face from its signification and subjectification and thus to elude its own abstract-machine. The cinema, in short, offers us the means by which to *lose face*, to circumvent the process whereby the face is collapsed into an identity, such that instead, it vibrates as a pure quality. The cinema holds out the prospect of a kind of duration whereby affection ceases to be the precedent to movement, to action, to determination and becomes 'irreducible to all realization', yet no less real (Deleuze, 2001: 106).

'The close-up does indeed suspend individuation', Deleuze writes in *Cinema 1*, but far from lamenting this eventuality, he and Guattari celebrate it as the basis of a practice and politics of the face. For by suspending individuation – or, more accurately, by liberating affect from the individual – we begin the process of annihilating the network of power relations with which the face has been determined, namely, signification and subjectification. At the end of the trajectory of the face that we have traced to this point, perhaps we can now say that the face is not only the locus of concepts (the Other Person complex), of affects (the close-up) and of politics (faciality), but that it enjoys its place in all of these domains (philosophy, cinema, schizoanalysis) because it is the locus of a problem to which each turns in turn. In each case, we could add, the face augurs not only a possible world but, also, the possibility of becoming-imperceptible. Deleuze's ubiquitous question, in so many different respects and of so many different domains, asks 'how we can get rid of ourselves?' If the face offers an answer, this is because it proffers the possibility of becoming anonymous. It is possible for a face to lose itself, to slough off its identity, but in so doing the affects that traverse it and that drain us of individuation achieve a kind of singularity: a feeling, a sensation, an intensity. The anecdote with which Deleuze describes this process, and with which we will conclude, derives from Ingmar Bergman's *Persona*. The film famously revolves around a kind of collective schizophrenia that grips its protagonists, Elisabet Voelger (Liv Ullmann) and Nurse Alma (Bibi Anderson). The former, a well-known actress, finds herself unable to complete a recent performance (she was playing Electra), and in the three months following this event she has not spoken a word. Nurse Alma is assigned to care for Elisabet, first at the sanitarium where she is recovering and thereafter at a sea-side cottage. It is in this seemingly isolated locale that the two begin to undergo a strange double-displacement, each woman unmoored from herself, drifting into a zone of indiscernibility. Who is the actress? Are both of them acting?

The abstract machine of faciality projects faces, but the cinematic machine realizes a different or schizoanalytic project: to slough off the face. As Deleuze writes, 'One need only recall that the actor himself does not recognize himself in the close-up (according to Bergman, "we were setting out to do some cutting and editing and Liv said: look at Bibi, she's awful! And Bibi said in turn: no, it's not me, it's you . . .")' (Deleuze, 1986: 103). Indeed, Bergman makes an abstract machine with two faces, but in the calculated alteration of plans sequences and close-ups, the film ultimately makes these indistinguishable. Notably, the film's 'narrative' is preceded by a surreal sequence of images – of a projector spewing film, of fragmented images of sex and torture – that culminates with a strange scene: in a hospital room, a lanky boy rises from an uncomfortable bed, finally turning to an enormous screen poised on a wall in front of him. On this screen is projected the enormous close-up of a face – first Elisabet's, until it slowly dissolves into Alma's and vice versa. Facing us, the face dopplers between these two poles while the boy faces the face, his back turned away from the camera and his awkward body framed in darkness against the bright surface: white wall, black hole – but in the absence of signification or subjectivity. With gentle timidity, the boy moves his silhouetted hand across the modulating face, as if to grasp a becoming that cannot be grasped but only felt, cannot be apprehended but only intuited. Of *Persona*, Bergman once said, he had 'touched wordless secrets that only the cinema can discover' (Vermiye, 123), but it seems to us that these secrets, which belong to schizoanalysis as much as to cinema, begin with the face.

Chapter 4

Disorientation, Duration and Tarkovsky

Mark Riley

Schizoanalysis as the analysis of desire, is immediately practical and political, whether it is a question of an individual group or society. For politics
precedes being. Practice does not come after the implacement of the terms
and their relations, but actively participates in *the drawing of lines*; it confronts the same dangers and same variations as the emplacement does.
Schizoanalysis is like the art of the new (Deleuze and Guattari, 1996: 204, my
emphasis).

This chapter seeks to navigate a nomadic/errant trip through the variant
articulations found in Andrei Tarkovsky's films, *Solaris* and *Stalker*.[1] It will
negotiate a journey directed by Deleuze and Guattari's conception of
nomadic thought and Deleuze's writings on cinema and the time-image
and seek to recognize an exteriority that resists the ordered interiority of
the restrictive analogical metaphysical edifice in favour of a freer movement of boundless conductivity.

Both *Solaris* and *Stalker* offer interpretations of an open-ended 'smooth
space' of nomadism – the surface of the planet Solaris and the 'zone' in
Stalker. Brian Massumi indicates that this process 'sums up a set of disparate
circumstances . . . synthesises a multiplicity of elements without effacing
their heterogeneity or hindering their potential for rearranging' (1992: 6).

Both films also offer an opportunity to consider the primary force of
'desire' in relation to its interpretation as a free-floating energy that is 'pure
multiplicity' and 'irreducible to any sort of unity' (Deleuze and Guattari,
1983: 50). This is manifest in the relationship between the characters of
Kelvin and Hari in *Solaris* and the collective experience of the 'scientist',
'writer' and the stalker in relation to 'the room' in *Stalker*. The nomadic
mode of distribution of 'smooth space' also links to the reappraisal of the
subordination of temporality to movement and the spatial that Deleuze
identifies in *Cinema 1* and *Cinema 2*. It identifies a plane of immanence as
an indeterminate schizophrenic field of possibilities 'in which' and 'by
which' possibilities are created. As Gregory Flaxman notes:

Schizophrenia expresses a 'possibility of thought' that lies in the aboli-
tion of the dogmatic image – a possibility that as such, also lies at the
heart of modern cinema and its derealisation of illusions. (2000: 46)

In *Cinema 1* and *Cinema 2* Deleuze attempts to transform film theory
into a philosophy whose rigour is localized and reflects the emergence of
rules that are immanent to each given zone of indetermination. Such a
system is essentially the affirmation of the schizophrenic; poised between
order and chaos. It does not give order or stamp an authority on chaos, but
delicately navigates the rift between. The schizoanalytic power of cinema is
found in this operation. It is neither 'beginning' nor 'end' but a 'between'
of invention, creativity and unpredictability.

In exiling us from the familial conceptual terrain and leading us to the
prospect of a 'becoming system', it indicates a certain kind of cinematic
aesthetic or systemization, through 'temporal de-coordination' – a kind of
disorientation. This is where the prospect of action (no longer merely
(re)action) of the futural is saturated by the past and raises the question;
how might we orientate ourselves in this flow of 'deterritorialisation'?[2]
Temporal de-coordination implies the interruptive distortion of aesthetic
representation through plurality and divergence. It is the recognition of
a superposition of perspectives and a tangle of viewpoints which, in a temporal sense, reveal a coexistence of moments. This labyrinthine 'view' is
arguably an interpretation of modern cinema. The conflagration of non-
linear relations, which Deleuze identifies in his interpretation of the
'crystal-image' in *Cinema 1* and *Cinema 2*, are determined cinematically, for
example, through the temporal bifurcation of *flashback*. (See Bogue, 1989:
116): 'What we see in flashbacks are the *residual traces* of a branching time,
the actual paths taken of a virtually forking labyrinth of coexisting paths.' It
is this bifurcating maze of time that gives the flashback their inner logic,
their 'necessity', their 'reason'. This operates outside the conventional
chronology of a commonsense through a figurative leap from the actuality
of the present into the virtuality of the past.

The fusion of the 'pastness' of a recorded event with the presentness of
its viewing is the indivisible unity of virtual image and actual image. This
understands the virtual as subjective or in the past – a 'pure recollection'
that exists outside consciousness in time but somewhere in a temporal
past, and which is still alive and ready to be recalled by the actual. What is
important to an understanding of the crystal-image is the fragmentariness
implied by the crystalline.[3] The past/presentness of the cinematic image
functions as a kind of two-way mirror. It operates as a fluctuation between

virtual and actual, splitting the screen into two heterogeneous directions – launching into the future *and* falling into the past. This arguably presents a schizophrenic confusion of mental and physical time. As Deleuze notes in *Cinema 2*:

> There is no present which is not haunted by a past and a future, by a past which is not reducible to a former present, by a future which does not consist of a present to come. (1989: 37)

Deleuze introduces a concept of *any-spaces-whatever (espaces quel-conque)* that indicates a new cinematic pedagogy: a disruption of the unity of space by drawing attention to the disparate scissions that fragment it. Flaxman notes in the introduction to *The Brain Is the Screen* that:

> These 'any-spaces-whatever' . . . irrational, disconnected, aberrant, *schizophrenic spaces* – no longer obey laws of traditional, commonsensical causality. At every turn, the hope for resolution is frustrated. (2000: 5, my emphasis)

The passage from virtual to actual is affected by what Deleuze terms 'an intensity' – the essential activity of energizing individuation. Metastability and intensity are states of *pre-sense*, in that they are essentially outside *commonsense* and cognitive understanding. As such, they can only be experienced in the disjunctive use of the faculties and distortion of the senses in moments of disequilibrium and vertigo. The concept of cinema is no longer defined as 'an undertaking of recognition', but 'a science of visual impressions, forcing us to forget our own logic and retinal habits' (Deleuze, 1989: 18–19). For Deleuze, thought begins with a contradictory experience – an encounter with a *simulacrum*. This encounter must take account of the simulacrum having 'no identity' – it is the manifestation of *difference in itself* and can only appear in disguise as distinct categories of individuation, which mask pre-individual, metastable differences.

Tarkovsky's cinematic adaptation of Stanislaw Lem's science-fiction novel, *Solaris* offers a specific cinematic vision of the simulacrum. In both film and book, the visitors are simulacra formed from the subconscious/memories of the surviving crewmembers of a space station orbiting the planet Solaris. Proximity to the planet and its ocean plays a significant part in the manifestation of these visitors, and links the specificity of individual memory to the realization of an influential pre-individual condition manifest in the planet itself. The visitors as simulacra could be understood as disguised distinct categories of individuation disguising/masking the pre-individual, metastable state of the planet Solaris and its ocean.

Each film, we might say is like an astronaut crew's exploration of a multi-faceted, gemlike planet. The crewmembers orbit the planet, taking various shots of its surface. They land, traverse different planes, then penetrate the planet's outer surfaces and film shimmering and prismatic reflections from within the planet, the facets of changing tints, growing foggy, opalescent, silvery or transparent. They follow the process of crystallization as a seed crystal spreads into a milieu; they record the shattering of a facet, the powdery disintegration of another, the liquid dissolution of a third (Bogue, 2003: 124).

The planet as an intermediary can only communicate with the scientists through the various visitations of the simulacra. In the film Kelvin's psychological dilemma is more clearly defined when he can no longer distinguish between the simulacra and the real/historical [present-ness and past] Hari [his wife]. Kelvin's 'visitor' becomes a manifestation of an intensity of his memory and has no identity of its own. It is unable to exist except in proximity to him – relying on him to form its identity. Kelvin's commonsense tells him that this phenomena is *not* his wife and crucially, also not *spectral.*

Scientifically, the visitor is defined as something beyond atomic structure and the corporeal – the realm of the *neutrino,* constituted of sub-atomic material and its capability for endless rejuvenation.[4] This realization that the visitor is more than just a *spectre* makes its manifestation all the more fearful. In the novel, Lem notes:

> When it arrives, the visitor is almost blank – only a *ghost* made up of memories and vague images dredged out of its . . . source. The longer it stays with you, the more human it becomes. It also becomes more independent, up to a certain point. (2003: 157)

The visitor *is* a 'body', in that it assumes a bodily form and in so doing disguises its difference through corporeality. It also exists as a surface to the *body* of Kelvin on the space station – a temporal/ephemeral attribute of the infinite. The visitor could be interpreted as the surface meaning of incorporeal on the corporeal Kelvin's visitor/wife is the realization of an incorporeal event from his past.[5] It/she is not only a 'product' of Solaris, but is also an effect of Kelvin's proximity to the planet. For it to exist, Kelvin as a body (a corporeal event) needs to be close to the planet. In this sense, Solaris could be construed as a transcendental pre-sense that precedes the 'corporeal' Kelvin and the 'incorporeal' Hari.

Kelvin attempts to instigate 'good sense' as that which underlines truth through science; that truth being that Hari cannot 'exist' as she has previously 'died'. Her/its presence on the space station is not a 'corporeal present of finitude', but an 'incorporeal infinitude' of how she is/was as recollected by Kelvin. The visitor is a simulacrum of the historical Hari projected by Solaris via the particularity and specificity of Kelvin's recollection – a fragmentary, proximal facsimile capable of a kind of evolution based in Kelvin's memory. The complication manifest in the realization of the visitor is in the recognition that the duality of interior/exterior is undermined. The visitor determines a differentiation that refuses to sustain any clear duality. Its manifestation is the interaction of a multiplicity and therefore can no longer be interpreted as the action of the subjective upon the objective. Kelvin's proximity to the planet determines his subjective priority in the relation, and the appearance of Hari as a specific historical manifestation substantiates such an interpretation. However, Solaris could also be seen as that which articulates this event and from which the realization of the visitor takes place.[6]

Kelvin recognizes the visitor as a facsimile of his wife but the disruption of his memory is heightened by her provisional blankness. As their relationship evolves, the visitor's memories are filled in by proximity to Kelvin. However, the most significant 'recollection' (Hari's suicide) remains a disturbance of memory until the visitor re-enacts the suicide. Each time it is rejuvenated, its memory/recollections of the real Hari expand so that although the seemingly infinite capacity of the visitor to regenerate itself indicates a kind of corporeal stasis (an eternal return of the body), the temporally linked aspect of memory is continually changing and in flux. This is most clearly identified when the visitor repeats the real Hari's attempt at suicide through the ingestion of liquid oxygen. This happens as the visitor accumulates more and more memory data through proximity to Kelvin, and therefore becomes familiar with the psychological trauma from Kelvin's past and which drove the 'real' Hari to end her life. Recollection is indiscriminate in that the facsimile cannot choose which memories inform its development in Kelvin's presence, and equally the planet's involvement does not differentiate good memory from bad and poses the question; is the visitor a 'good' or a 'bad' copy – a *phantasme?*

Kelvin does not act as merely the 'source' of the simulacra but rather also as the 'point of view' from which the simulacra might be viewed – the screen.[7] The effect of the simulacra as a spectral manifestation of memory would suggest that in a way Hari is already immanent as a problem within Kelvin in two aspects; first, as a transcendental ground of possible actualizations and second, as a secondary effect or simulacrum. The visitor could be conceived as a point of immanence specified by the proximity of the corporeal Kelvin and, most importantly, his memory of his wife at the time of her death, to the pre-individuation manifest in Solaris as a kind of transcendental ground.

The ability of the planet to continually replicate Hari illustrates and articulates the notion that at the heart of infinity is repetition. Each 'new' Hari is physically the same as the previous one (a simulation of Kelvin's recollection of her at the time of her physical death), and clearly that sameness is based in Kelvin's memory as interpreted by Solaris. That sameness is inherently different from the source Hari. Solaris creates this particular visitor not from a first-hand or ideal person, but from the memory of another (Kelvin) whose recollective idiosyncrasies must inform the simulation. The implication here is that repetition is not grounded in similitude as a replication understood through sameness, but that it is contingent on an essential difference.[8] This paradox of meaning suggests a link between *after-effect* and something that is always already there but which is also a transcendental condition of possible meanings and becomings. In linguistic terms, the ideal matter of words is essentially not lingual and the singular point of things is not essentially physical, but suggests centres of *virtual* difference before being explicated or actualized in specific forms. This indicates what we might term a 'transcendental field' of *both* meaning *and* events, which suggests a metaphysical surface that is manifest in paradox and simulacra.

The capacity for the planet to read and interpret memory does not include an ability to differentiate between what might be considered a 'good' or a 'bad' recollection for the one visited, increasing the possibility of a kind of undifferentiated repetition steeped in the potential trauma of the original relationship. In the novel, the character Snow interprets the process by which the planet manifests the phenomenon of the visitors as one that 'probed our brains and penetrated to some kind of psychic tumour' (Lem, 2003: 77).[9] In the same passage he states that it:

> isolated psychic processes, enclosed, stifled, encysted – foci smouldering under the ashes of memory. It deciphered them and made use of them, in the same way one uses a recipe or blueprint. (Lem, 2003: 77)

The amoral condition of an outside agency is explored again by Tarkovsky in *Stalker*.[10] The 'object of desire' of the travellers – the room at the centre of 'the zone' is not merely amoral, but outside the framework 'by which' and 'for which' morality can stake a claim. The stalker identifies the risk of the wish-fulfilment aspect of the room, not through the consciousness of such wishing but through the unconscious desires of the travellers. What remains intolerable about the room is that it represents unbearable possibility.

Interpreting the stalker as a 'schizophrenic visionary' or 'far-seer' situates him outside the nihilistic conception of 'desire as lack', resonating with Deleuze and Guattari's interpretation of 'desire' as pre-personal and pre-individual. The stalker is not caught up in the status of his role, and continually underplays his worthiness, yet it is he who is seemingly granted his 'unconscious wish' as he is uncontaminated by a corrupted/conscious desire and adrift (unlike 'Writer' and particularly 'Scientist', whose intent is to destroy the room with an explosive device so as to extinguish false hope in others).

For Deleuze and Guattari, schizophrenics are 'adrift' in a capitalist society centred on the psychoanalytic neurosis of the Oedipal family. Objects and things become a collection of dissociated body parts, dismembered, interpenetrating – a Body without Organs. Schizophrenics are both outside of social mechanisms and organized by their codes. They are 'beyond' the bounds of sense. Incorporeal non-sense functions for Deleuze as the structuring force of the transcendental field of singular points and is a stable intrinsic meaning that can never be found in mere deferral. In *Stalker*, the character of the stalker is blessed with the idiocy of a kind of schizophrenia. He negotiates the zone by finding paths with a topological pre-sense founded in the adaptability of his experience and intuition, and takes charge of the *rational* and *scholastic* (identified in his fellow travellers, 'Writer' and 'Scientist').

Mark Le Fanu suggests that Tarkovsky presents the stalker as 'a holy fool' who expresses himself through gesture. For Tarkovsky, cinema has become a quasi-silent medium and the stalker's vulnerability resists being pinned down.

In sum, *he is opaque and ungraspable* – an apparition (Le Fanu, 1990: 98, my emphasis).

In *Cinema 2*, Deleuze also elucidates a new kind of ambiguous character that inhabits cinema. In *A Thousand Plateaus*, Deleuze and Guattari propose someone they refer to as 'a far-seer':

> It is because what happens to them does not belong to them and only half concerns them, because they know how to extract from the 'event' the part that cannot be reduced to what happens: that part of inexhaustible

possibility that constitutes the unbearable, the intolerable, the visionary's part. (Deleuze, 1989: 19–20)[11]

Le Fanu argues that Tarkovsky's extended close-up of the stalker's face in the zone resists the anticipation of a profound oration in favour of a study of vulnerability. Rather than resort to mere pathos, this emphasizes the opaqueness of the protagonist. In this sense, the anticipation of possible readings of the character mirrors the navigation of 'the zone' (a reading on the stalker's face of the uncertainty of the possible directions that might be taken – a view of the landscape). In *A Thousand Plateaus*, Deleuze and Guattari argue:

> The close-up in film treats the face as a landscape: that is the definition of film, black hole and white wall, screen and camera. (Deleuze and Guattari, 1996: 172)[12]

The face reflects the stratification of the landscape. Links can be made across strata, where newness and the untimely transgress established stratifications in shifts which open up new fault lines and possibilities through the continual event of mutation. The cinematic resonance of this conception of temporality and montage should not be lost, and the pertinence of complication as the overarching thematic at work is further articulated by the reconsideration of sense and event as the motivation of thought, rather than the historical imperatives of truth and proposition. In *Cinema 1* Deleuze states:

> The cinematographic image is always dividual. This is because, in the final analysis, the screen, as the frame of frames, gives a common standard of measurement to things which do not have one – long shots of countryside and close-ups of the face, an astronomical system and a single drop of water – parts which do not have the same denominator of distance, relief or light. In all these senses the frame ensures a deterritorialisation of the image. (Deleuze, 1997: 14–15)

This is a *geophilosophy* that rethinks borders based on odd potentials, different circumstances and contingencies rather than origins – a deterritorialization as 'nowhere', not covered or compensated by an imagined community or utopian condition. What matters are the differences of orientation that suggest the image of thought operates as a kind of mapping. This is no longer a 'negation' in the sense of something erroneous to be corrected or overcome, rather a stupidity to be exposed and attacked. Stupidity suggests any philosophical conflict not based in a propositional error of ideality, but in taking on the intractable, not as irrational but as involving the thinker in a relation with something arguably inhuman and intolerable.

Deleuze argues that the navigation of space refuses any traditional concept of mapping and posits a condition of filling out. This refutes any determination towards unrestrained organization while also indicating the inseparability of space and movement. Modern cinema differs from classical cinema because it pulverizes chronology so that the temporal is no longer subordinate to the integrity of movement as mere physical actions, but remains fragmented like the parts of a broken crystal. This proposes the cinematic 'shot' as essentially open and variable.

Modern cinema proffers the discontinuity of the irrational as the means by which the smooth running of any variation on movement as essentially continuous and legible is undermined. The breakdown of what Deleuze calls the sensor-motor system happens when direct action and reaction are undermined by the discontinuity of temporal shifts and the appearance of vacant and disconnected spaces ('any-space-whatevers' – the planet Solaris or the zone), which disrupt continuity and push the characters into more passive roles.

As already suggested, this pre-geometric spatiality is essentially transgressive and schizophrenic. It escapes striated division and topographic determination to exploit intensities beyond the limit of the lived body of phenomenological properties. The shift in cinema is, for Deleuze, a slackening of sensory-motor connections, replacing them with purely optical and sound situations. He argues: 'in the adult world, the child is affected by a certain motor helplessness, but one which makes him all the more capable of seeing and hearing' (Deleuze, 1989: 3).

In *Stalker*, the stalker's child illustrates a pre/post sensory condition that is not only heightened by her motor helplessness (it is made explicit that she literally cannot walk) but also, as indicated at the end of the film, by the fact that she is telepathic – perhaps a gift/curse of the zone/room.

There is an implication in both film and novel[13] that the stalker's forays into the zone (and resulting contamination) are responsible for the child's condition. The trip which takes place in Tarkovsky's cinematic adaptation indicates that an unconscious desire/wish is fulfilled by the room on the stalker's return, in that it appears that the child is now mobile. However, it is later revealed that she is in fact 'walking' on her father's shoulders.[14]

The possibilities inherent in this slippage recognize the 'between' of any formal genres as integral to a new understanding of how a structure might be recognized. It identifies 'complication' and 'interruption' as the essential schematic of mutability.

It opened up possibilities for recreating in a new way the true atmosphere of war, with its hyper-tense nervous concentration, invisible on the surface of events but making itself felt like a rumbling beneath the ground (Tarkovsky, 1986: 17).

Deleuze suggests that Tarkovsky's interpretation of time and how it flows through the shot is essentially through tension and rarefaction – the pressure of time in the shot. He argues that Tarkovsky denied the notion of a language of cinema working with units – the distinction between 'shot' as a framing device for the temporal, and 'montage', which articulates and expresses the pressure of time to exceed the limits of any shot. If matter were already image in the sense of a fundamental appearing, it becomes luminous in that all that could be perceived would be already inherent as the replete state of the image. Deleuze refers to this condition as the 'plane of immanence' and this is essentially virtual to the extent that the requirements of the corporeal (the body) demand that limits are put in place on what can actually be apprehended in matter.

Matter and image are continuous with yet distinct from human perception on the understanding that the picturing of matter limits via its human/corporeal role and acts as a filter which relays specific information on specific wavelengths. This indicates two systems of images: one that is universal and immanent and the other that is bodily and filtered by the physiological limits and human requirements.

The unevenness that constitutes the spatio-temporal relation in the zone suggests a composite which articulates a combination allowing the spatial to introduce its forms of what Deleuze would term extrinsic distinctions of sectional homogeneous discontinuity, while duration contributes a kind of internal succession that is both heterogeneous and continuous. In *The Logic of Sense* Deleuze *explores* the idea that perpetual displacement and empty place combine through the experiential to transcend lived experience through a process of 'going beyond', which not only suggests an enlargement of that experience but proposes that such expansion is always and already a condition of that experience.

The room at the centre of the zone in *Stalker* and the oceans of Solaris permeate the consciousness of not only all who seek them or come into their proximity, but all who are aware of their mythologies – all who aspire to visit yet are fearful and uncertain of the risks involved in undertaking such a journey. The stalker's 'thread' and the attempts at scientific exactitude by the occupants of the space station in *Solaris* are predisposed to navigation while continually questioning the transcription of what appears to be navigable or seemingly requiring navigation. They explore the expansiveness of 'unimagined ways' and the becoming of 'smooth space' through the divination of the future from the past – the crystal-image.

Disorientation presents the quandary in which the combination of compression and release in the crystal-image are found. The continuous discontinuity of the labyrinthine – through a combination of disclosure and undisclosure marked by, and defining illumination *and* shadow, remains *other* to both. Orientation is always and already disoriented and interred in the rules of navigation as its secret arbiter. They are schizophrenic operations with which the aesthetic of the cinematic escapes the confinement of sequential spatiality through the temporal deterritorialization and discontinuity of fragmentation and as yet unknowable and unforeseen combinations. As Deleuze and Guattari note:

> The map is open and connectable in all its dimensions; it is detachable, reversible, susceptible to constant modification. It can be torn, reversed, adapted to any kind of mounting, reworked by any individual, group or social formation. It can be drawn on a wall, conceived as a work of art, constructed as a political action or as a meditation. (1996: 12)

Chapter 5

Suspended Gestures: Schizoanalysis, Affect and the Face in Cinema

Amy Herzog

Our work begins with the human face. . . . The possibility of drawing near to the . . . face is the primary originality and the distinctive quality of the cinema.[1]
—*Ingmar Bergman*

Gilles Deleuze thus invokes Bergman in the first volume of his *Cinema* books, in a chapter on affect and the face. Within these volumes, Deleuze borrows from Henri Bergson's theory of perception and time to craft a film-philosophy that opposes linguistic or psychoanalytic approaches to cinema. It seems somewhat peculiar, then, that Deleuze's discussion of affect centres upon the role of the face, a role he further links to that of the close-up. This move is anomalous for several reasons. Though the *Cinema* books chronicle a seemingly endless taxonomy of signs (e.g. perception-images, recollection-images, chronosigns, qualisigns), Deleuze is careful to avoid simple correlations between the theoretical concepts he discusses and concrete formal techniques. He further avoids readings of filmic content that might reduce the film-event to a static 'text' that could be decoded. The implied link between depictions of faces, the stylistic use of close-ups, and the generation of affective responses thus appears, on the surface, to be somewhat inconsistent with Deleuze's larger project.

Moreover, the association of the face with affect treads close to cognitive and psychological models, which typically read the face as a register of interior states, a means of both communicating and eliciting emotional reactions. If facial expressions are signs, this seems to suggest the presence of a subject whose face 'speaks' emotion, as well as a separate spectator-subject who reads and emotionally responds to the messages conveyed. Such a scenario seems entirely at odds with Deleuzian theory, which questions the notion of a coherent subject, opposes clear distinctions between interiority and exteriority and is deeply suspicious of the Saussurean split between signifier and signified, let alone the implication that one's face might transparently signify some truth about interior psychic states.

Deleuze's interest in the cinematic face is far more complex than it might initially appear. His references to faciality invoke a long history of fascination with the physiognomy of the close-up in film theory, in particular the writings of Jean Epstein and Béla Balázs. At the same time Deleuze's approach here intersects with his work with Félix Guattari on faciality, representation and structures of power in the *Capitalism and Schizophrenia* volumes. Given the centrality of the face to film theory, psychoanalysis, and Deleuze and Guattari's formulation of schizoanalysis, faciality seem a productive place to begin to imagine a schizoanalysis of cinema. If the face has traditionally been approached as a site for both the creation and expression of human subjectivity, schizoanalysis engages with faciality, particularly as it is deployed in the arts, to enact a provocative challenge to the systems that produce such subjects. Deleuze and Guattari write, 'Reading a text':

> is never a scholarly exercise in search of what is signified, still less a highly textual exercise in search of a signifier. Rather it is a productive use of the literary machine, a montage of desiring-machines, a schizoid exercise that extracts from the text its revolutionary force. (1983: 106)

Although Deleuze and Guattari specifically reference literature here, they are explicit about the centrality of artistic practice in general to their schizoanalytic project. This project rejects the reign of an expert analyst, a figure versed in the cloistered code of an institutionalized discourse who performs a diagnosis of the art-object-cum-analysand. Instead of a self-enclosed system of modelization (a system that presents a pre-formulated interpretative schema), schizoanalysis is an open 'meta-model' that can serve as 'an instrument for deciphering systems of modelization in various other fields' (Guattari, 1998: 433). Rather than interpreting pre-constituted subjects, schizoanalysis maps the nexus of forces that work to make subject formation possible. The goal is to expose the repressive operations of such systems, dismantling them and opening them to unforeseen connections with outside elements. The tools of schizoanalysis are inconsistent and continually evolving, arising, as they must, from their unique social and historical conditions. The key, for Guattari, is to seek out, within these social contexts, those assemblages of enunciation 'that are capable of fashioning new coordinates for reading and for "bringing to life" hitherto unknown representations and propositions' (Guattari, 1998: 433).

The arts are one of a constellation of social, technological, scientific and aesthetic fields through which schizoanalysis can work, bringing to light the connections and flows that constitute the machine of a social regime. Yet the arts occupy a privileged position, for while they are necessarily embedded within dominant political and economic systems, they nevertheless have the potential to deterritorialize, bursting open and extending beyond the system to forge new alliances. These new connections are expressive and creative, providing the basis for the assemblages of enunciation that, for Deleuze and Guattari, offer a means of political transformation.[2] A schizoanalysis of cinema, then, would not approach a film as a representational object to be analysed or decoded. Instead, schizoanalysis confronts the film-event as a machinic force, exploring the means by which 'collective arrangements' of filmic enunciation might function within, through, and against larger systems of social power. These systems, namely here the capitalist-familial regime, strive to reterritorialize and repress, to code and contain subjects according to pre-existing laws. As a corollary of this 'civilized capitalist machine', the film industry invariably produces works that reinforce the dominant values of that system. Yet film, as an art, is also a 'desiring-machine', one that produces affective expressions that are not always strictly coded, and which have the potential to deterritorialize (Deleuze and Guattari, 1983: 32). As Guattari writes:

> Commercial cinema is undeniably familialist, Oedipian, and reactionary. But it is not intrinsically so, the way psychoanalysis is. It is so 'on top of everything else'. Its 'mission' is not to adapt people to outdated and archaic elitist Freudian models, but to those implied by mass production . . . While its 'analytic' means are richer, more dangerous, because more fascinating than those of psychoanalysis, they are, in fact, more precarious and more full of promise. (1996: 165)

Cinema is not only firmly embedded within the capitalist power structure, it typically functions as one of that system's most potent tools of subjectification. Yet for Guattari, the language of cinema, unlike that of psychoanalysis, is 'alive', it contains, in its machinic excesses, the potential to challenge repressive systems and to 'modify the arrangements of desire' (1996: 165).

Schizoanalysis is thus engaged in a series of destructive and productive tasks. It must dismantle Oedipus, castration and other impediments to the 'flow of desire'. At the same time, schizoanalysis entails two productive activities. The first involves 'discovering in a subject the nature, the formation, or the functioning of *his* desiring-machines, independently of any interpretations' (Deleuze and Guattari, 1983: 322).[3] This task requires viewing the partial objects that comprise the parts of the desire-machines as they are dispersed, resisting the temptation to organize them under the rubric of a structural whole. The second task has to do with the revolutionary potential of a 'schizophrenic escape' (1983: 341). The goal here is not to leave the social context behind, for this would be impossible, but to couple escape with a social investment. This escape, which is more precisely a virtual potentiality, lies in the mapping of the 'machinic indices' of 'libidinal investments in the social field' (1983: 350). Schizoanalysis here creates breaks, schizzes that take up the flows of unconscious desire to 'resect them according to mobile and nonconfigurative points' (1983: 351). In relation to the face, then, a schizoanalytic approach first aims to dismantle the territorializing traits associated with the face as a representational and signifying entity. This dismantling in turn provides for a productive movement beyond repressive configurations towards new, creative assemblages. This potential movement must always be approached, however, as firmly embedded within the social. The line of flight is not an individual liberation: it is the schizophrenizing of a social regime.

The sections that follow will attempt to map the visage of faciality as it surfaces in a number of Deleuze's, and Deleuze and Guattari's texts, where each figure the face according to different modalities and artistic media. I will then turn to a film that deploys the face in a manner that resonates with both the destructive and productive functions of schizoanalysis, Pedro Almodóvar's *Bad Education* (2004).

Affect and faciality

The notion of affect, for Bergson, arises from an interval between perception and action. For both Deleuze and Bergson this interval is a 'center of indetermination', a delay brought about by the living being who subtracts from the chaotic swirl of images that comprise the world just those perceptions that are of interest, those things that the being can act upon, or which might act upon the being (Deleuze, 1986: 61). This delay or space marks the seat of lived existence, what Deleuze calls 'a coincidence of subject and object', a mixing of sensations from the outside and the experience of the being from the inside (1986: 65).

'Perception', Bergson writes, 'in its pure state, is, then, in very truth, a part of things. As for affective sensation, it does not spring spontaneously from the depths of consciousness to extend itself, as it grows weaker, in space; it is one with the necessary modifications to which, in the midst of the surrounding images that influence it, the particular image that each one of us terms his body is subject' (1991: 65). Living beings, then, are the contingent centres binding assemblages of perception-images, action-images and affection-images. Though the most immediate goals of any being are geared towards action, there is nevertheless a residue, an after-image that arises from the act perception – namely, elements of images not filtered into action. These images, distilled from their immediate context, are thus 'framed'; Deleuze describes them as 'isolated', part of 'closed systems' or 'tableaux' (1986: 61). Although the body as a whole may remain temporarily immobile or inactive within the space of the interval, there is a certain 'effort' generated in response to this after-image: affection. What we find with affect is that body movement is truncated and turned into expression, a movement of the sensorial capacities, and a temporal shift towards memory and the sheets of the virtual past.

Affective sensation, for Bergson, is a physiological, sensory response to what might otherwise be transmuted into outward physical movements. Deleuze describes the phenomenon as a 'motor effort on an immobilized receptive plate', a gestural expression of affect (1986: 66). He further suggests that this mode of expression is most clearly manifested on the face, leading to his rather curious assertion: 'the affection-image is the close-up, and the close-up is the face' (1986: 87).

The first point one should emphasize here is that Deleuze does not limit his discussion to the human face, and in fact stresses the manner in which all kinds of objects, landscapes and images are capable of being 'facialized' in film. The question here is not one of resemblance (an object that looks like a face), or an anthropomorphic subjectivity, but rather to ask what it is that faces *do* (see Rushton, 2002). There are two poles associated with what faces do, for Deleuze: one a reflective, unified surface, the other a multiplicity of parts that move, shifting between states, independently. Deleuze offers the example of a clock. When looking at the clock, one might focus one's attention on the incremental movements of the two hands – what we find here is an 'intensive series'. One could also focus on the face of the clock as a whole, a 'receptive immobile surface' (Deleuze, 1986: 87). Each of these qualities exists simultaneously, two 'conditions of possibility' that can either open through serial movements to connect with other worlds or occupy the reflective space of the interval (Rushton, 2002: 231). While the human face is clearly the nexus from which this notion of faciality emerges, Deleuze extends it into all manner of images that possess these poles: even that which does not resemble a face can be 'facified', and as such, look back at us (1986: 87–8).

Deleuze does not deny that the face, in our everyday encounters, serves to convey information in a number of capacities: it distinguishes one individual from another, it serves in a socializing capacity and it works to communicate information. Yet in the close-up, these capacities are 'dissolved', the face becomes a 'phantom', opaque, distilled from its spatio-temporal coordinates. As Balázs describes this process:

> [W]hen a face that we have just seen in the middle of a crowd is detached from its surroundings, put into relief, it is as if we were suddenly face to face with it. . . . Our sensation of space is abolished. A dimension of another order is opened to us. (Deleuze 1986: 96)

This abstraction, this lack of individuation is disquieting precisely because the face no longer functions in its everyday capacity as a situated, communicative interface. Stretched across the screen, the face is held immobile by the close-up, yet is animated and traversed by mobile expressive parts.[4] The decontextualized face confronts us with its impenetrable topography. Ungrounded, the face serves as sheer potentiality, a suspended gesture.[5]

What Deleuze associates with the face, then, can be extended to any type of shot that works to isolate and extract some kind of expressive quality in and for itself. In Peircean terms, the affection-image is associated with firstness, a 'quality of feeling' in itself, encountered with no outside reference – it is a state of possibility prior to any linkage in a system of signification, or to a sequence of action-reaction. For Deleuze, this abstraction of space can extract a kind of 'faciality' from all kinds of images (parts of the body, objects, landscapes) with an expressive intensity. The question is not merely one of form. Deleuze argues that shots that are not technically 'close' can achieve the status of the close-up through the collapsing of depth, or 'the suppression of perspective', such that the image elicits an affective power or quality (1986: 107); one might likewise presume that some technically close shots fail to perform as close-ups in this capacity. Thus while for Deleuze the close-up face in cinema may not exist as such in a literal sense. The quality of faciality and the function of the close-up is clearly that of pure affect.

The affection-image exists as a kind of tableau vivant, vibrating immobility, in a perpetual state of inbetween-ness. It becomes a sheer surface, a screen of potentiality with an extended duration that supplants action and agency (Deleuze, 1986: 99–100). The face as affection-image marks a threshold between worlds, a moment of forking time where various potential paths, actions and lines of flight transect.

Signification and subjectification

Although the facial encounter is indeed one of potential openness, this does not necessarily lead to the degree of destabilization that Deleuze associates with the time-image. Indeed, one must read the discussion of the face in the *Cinema* books in the context of Deleuze's collaborations with Guattari. In *A Thousand Plateaus*, Deleuze and Guattari discuss the face as central to the twinned processes of signification and subjectification, a means of centralizing, classifying and enforcing systems of power. This function of faciality is not universal; it is engendered by particular social regimes based on their configurations of meaning, rule and power. Deleuze and Guattari outline several types of social regimes in relation to this question of faciality (a list, which they clarify, is not exhaustive). Polyvocal 'primitive' societies are relatively decentralized, and while there is certainly a level of symbolization at work, it, too, remains localized, corporeal and open to transmutations. The signifying regime, however, centralizes power with the state. The body of the despot-leader stands in for the body of the state, and the leader's face becomes the signifying centre from which all meaning radiates. All signs are filtered through this face, and interpretation (embodied in the figure of the priest) spirals outwards in rings of decreasing conformity. In art-historical terms, as Ronald Bogue illustrates, we might envision the despotic face as the icon of Christ Pantocrator, omnipotent, facing directly forward, encircled by a halo, or gazing down from the summit of a dome (2003: 96). Counter to the face of the despot is the body of the tortured, the scapegoat who loses his/her face, and whose line of flight, in that first step before exclusion, marks the entropy of the system, that which resists signification, everything that is 'bad' (Deleuze and Guattari, 1987: 116).

The post-signifying regime, by contrast, is marked by a recuperation of the scapegoat's line of flight, rerouting it into 'into the positive line of our subjectivity, our Passion' (Deleuze and Guattari, 1987: 122). The figure of the wandering prophet embodies this figure, driven by passion rather than interpretation. The relationship to the face of the despot shifts here; there is a turning away – God averts his face, and the subject turns away in fear (1987: 123). This is the regime of betrayal – the people betray God, but in doing so, fulfil God's wishes by taking evil unto themselves, enacting, as such a double betrayal. We find ourselves here confronted not with a central governing face, the face seen from the front as with the Byzantine icon, but rather by 'a face-off between two countenances that become gaunt and turn away in profile' (1987: 124).[6] We might look here to the semi-averted gazes in Duccio's *The Calling of Saint Peter and Saint Andrew*, or the faces of Christ and Judas, eyes locked, frozen in direct profile among the backdrop of the crowd in Giotto's *The Kiss of Judas*. This is the point of subjectification, a vortex, a site of de- and reterritorialization that gives rise to the subject of enunciation, as well as the subject of statement. Deleuze and Guattari compare this to the analysand in psychoanalysis, who is always subject to the discourse she speaks, or rather which speaks through her, whereas the analyst never has to speak at all (1987: 129–32). These various regimes, for Deleuze and Guattari, almost always exist in mixed states. The face that governs the mixed despotic-passional regime is not just any face, but rather the white wall/black hole system that Deleuze and Guattari link historically with the year zero (1987: 182). Rather than a concrete face, we find at the heart of this system an abstract machine that performs the integrated processes of signification and subjectification through the mask of the White Man par excellence, as Deleuze and Guattari describe him, 'Jesus Christ superstar' (1987: 176). The empty black hole of this face is a machine that blindly evaluates the faces that pass before it, computing degrees of deviation and gridding the subjects that pass through it. In other words, the face as a signifying and subjectifying entity is the product of an abstract system, one that constitutes that face as a means of individuation, categorization and identification according to a matrix of surveillance, power and control. Race is central to this system, and hence Deleuze and Guattari's insistence that this facializing machine be described as a *white* wall with gaping black holes, a system with deep historical, political and geographical roots, through and against which all other faces are organized and defined. The white wall/black hole system overcodes, or facializes, not just subjects but the world; it is programmed to obviate the presence of an outside through an unending series of signifying chains, all hurtling towards the depthless black hole of subjectivity (1987: 179).

There is another entity that can be born from the excesses of the facial machine, a 'probe-head', like an automated missile, that functions to defacialize, to deterritorialize and as such to create new transversals between different traits and strata (Deleuze and Guattari, 1987: 190). We might look here to an artist such as Francis Bacon. Bacon draws forth the head, the body, obscured by the face, the 'meat', unleashing a realm of indeterminate, animal fleshiness. The point is not merely to abstract or deform, but to touch a nerve, to illuminate the resonances between bodies obscured by our representational regimes. This returns to the question of affect:

'The affect is not the passage from one lived state to another but man's nonhuman becoming. . . . It is a zone of indetermination, of indiscernibility, as if things, beasts, and persons . . . endlessly reach that point that immediately precedes their natural differentiation' (Deleuze and Guattari, 1994: 173).[7] In light of the involution of signification and subjectivity that Deleuze and Guattari link to the face, we might thus locate within the affection-image two tendencies: one towards the kind of facialization that imposes order, that grids the subject, and the other towards a deterritorialization of the face that counters the subject as well as the larger system of representation. An interrogation of the face would thus require the same destructive and productive tasks associated with schizoanalysis, a tearing down, and an excavation, accompanied by a movement outwards:

> Dismantling the face is the same as breaking through the wall of the signifier and getting out of the black hole of subjectivity. Here, the program, the slogan, of schizoanalysis is: Find your black holes and white walls, know your faces; it is the only way you will be able to dismantle them and draw your lines of flight. (Deleuze and Guattari, 1987: 188)

'The face, what a horror', Deleuze and Guattari write. 'It is naturally a lunar landscape, with its pores, planes, matts . . . and holes: there is no need for a close-up to make it inhuman; it is naturally a close-up, and naturally inhuman' (1987: 190). Indeed the face, as affection-image, is a block of sensation. Much like Bacon's paintings use colour, rhythm and the figural to make visible new corporeal relations, the cinematic face harnesses its own specific qualities (duration, movement and configurations of space), to unleash an expressive force. This focus on sensation, affect and a not-necessarily-human corporeality forms the clearest link between these two distinct, but overlapping presentations of the face: the decontextualizing face found in the *Cinema* books, and the primitive-head/Christ-face/Probe-head figures in *A Thousand Plateaus*.[8] As a plateau between perception and action, a threshold for both signification and subjectivity, the face is central to the schizoanalytic project.

Beneath the gaze of the father: *Bad Education*

It would be a mistake to read Deleuze and Guattari's work on faciality in a literal sense, focusing too closely on concrete human faces, rather than on structures of power. The reason they choose to describe this process as 'facialization', rather than a more abstract term, is because it is with the human face that we initially and most overtly engage in these processes. With this in mind, I would like to reflect on a film that explores precisely this dynamic: Pedro Almodóvar's *Bad Education*. There is a level on which the work re-enacts the trauma of the despotic-passional regime. There are clear visual parallels to the kinds of facial relationships Deleuze and Guattari describe, as well as thematic resonances. What is at stake here, beyond the concrete depictions of the face, its visual distortions, or the narrative content, is the deployment of sensations that excavate the forces and networks that define a particular moment. Almodóvar explores the relations between faces as a means of illuminating the physiognomy of the fascist-Catholic regime, and excavating the pervasive, lingering microfascisms still registered in the visage of post-Franco Spain.

Bad Education is comprised of several versions of a narrative nested within one another, as Almodóvar describes them, like Russian dolls.[9] The heart of the story involves two young boys, Ignacio and Enrique, who fall in love while students at a Catholic boarding school in 1964. Ignacio has become the obsession of his literature teacher, Father Manolo, who ceaselessly preys upon him. Manolo, unable to possess the object of his desire, is consumed with jealousy, and expels Enrique from the school, severing the boys' relationship. This story is presented to us in a highly mediated fashion; however, the present day of the film is 1980, where the adult Enrique, who is now a film director, is visited by an actor who claims to be Ignacio, who gives him a story, '*The Visit*', based on their childhood experiences. The tale unfolds through a web of narrated 'visits' and texts (written, filmic and verbal), each revealing enfolded layers of betrayal, impersonation and falsification.

The polyphonic layers in the film are comprised of stylized tableaux, each fixated on the performance of the face. Faciality in this context is explicitly relational. We see the frontal face of the child as a love object, gazing at length directly into the camera. We see as well the averted face of betrayal and shame, the face of lust, and, like a true film noir, the exchange of recognition and affection between faces that will be undone by a darker unmasking (assisted, in one instance, by digital effects, as the faces of the boys metamorphose into what we assume to be their adult countenances). We see the face of the filmic icon, Sara Montiel, in a coquettish 3/4 view, floating on a theatre screen above the silhouettes of the young boys, who pleasure each other beneath her benevolent gaze. Montiel's face is revisited in the performances of her imitators, the aging drag queen and the imposter Ignacio, who remains still the visage of desire. Most pervasively, we see the confrontation in profile that marks each visit. Almodóvar presents an endless profusion of such shots, where each character 'faces off' the other in stark, perfectly centred direct profiles highly reminiscent of Giotti's *Judas*. We find here as well a 'facefication' of surfaces (walls, posters, statues, text), sometimes nearly literal, unleashing a 'looking back' that seems palpable even to the characters. The climax of this attention to the face occurs when Ignacio is violated by the priest, resulting in a fundamental split; as a stream of blood flows down his forehead, the image itself rends open, tearing his face in two.

The face here, which is in fact a face constructed through the adult Ignacio's written story, proffered by the figure of Ignacio's brother and impostor, visualized through the adult Enrique's film version, becomes a surface, a wall on which the story is written and a vortex into which sub-jectivity spins. It is a marker of time as well, its torn surface echoing the ripped layers of the movie posters that form the strata of history in the film. The encounter with the face is always a performance, a fact that Almodóvar emphasizes not only through the framed narrative, but also through the proscenium of the screen itself, whose aspect ratio slides open and closed like curtains around the image throughout the course of the film.

There is another type of face that emerges within this context. Beyond the human face, the only other image that sustains such close attention within the film is that of the written word. As Ignacio's tale unfolds through its many written iterations, the characters, and the camera, repeatedly fall into the face of the typewritten page. The text itself becomes another kind of white wall/black hole system, shot in a manner that echoes the exchanges between faces, rendered with a sensuous tactility. The written page is often the force that sets the stage for a 'visit', and is treated by the camera in much the same way as the human face, in consuming frontal close-ups, and in paired encounters, in profile. Signification and subjectifi-cation occur here, but in the same manner in which the relations between faces are dissected by the image, the text here, too, falls into fabulation far more often than it reveals the truth.

Thus while the face, in all its incarnations in *Bad Education*, might not go so far as to dismantle the power-relations that govern the despotic-passional regime, it brings to light the perversion that lies at the heart of the machine. The machine that is interrogated here is a very specific one, rooted in its cultural context. The narrative does not make its political grounding fully explicit, yet the carefully plotted temporal settings (the childhood trauma in 1964, Ignacio's story set in 1977 and the present-day film production set in 1980) mark key moments in Spanish history. Almodóvar's project is far more political than it is religious. From behind the Christ-face, the visage that governs this system is clearly that of Franco. It seems key to note, as well, the regime of cinema that maintains a spectral presence throughout the film, registered within the mercurial ambitions of Ignacio's actor-brother, the schizoid pleasures of the queer-queen-mother Sarah Montiel, as well as in Enrique's (and Almodóvar's) position as author. Clearly such systems, like the narrative, are folded into one another.

If the passional regime centres upon the point of subjectification, within Almodóvar's passion play that point is subverted and multiplied. Deterritorialization is not complete. (We remain grounded in the character of Enrique, the singular 'real' identity, the recipient of the final, albeit incomplete, textual communication from his lover and the partial, if unreliable double for the writer/director Almodóvar himself.) What is significant, however, is the painstaking manner in which these positions and relationships are exhumed, and the role which affect plays in suspending, bifurcating and redirecting the trajectory of action. The complex interactions between signification, adoration, subject formation and systems of control are unraveled through assemblages of faces and their myriad affects.

In exploring this multifaceted potential of faciality – a genealogical exploration of history, paired with a force propelling towards change and futurity – *Bad Education* deploys the face in ways that undermine restrictive presentations of subjectivity and identity, interior and exterior. Simultaneously, through its various performative iterations, falsifications and resonations with its environment, the face is rent open to new trans-subjective alliances. The film achieves this not by asserting a universal sensation, a common denominator emotion, but by exposing the repressive system through which subjects' faces and sensations are coded. This is not a flight into pure abstraction but a slow, painful process of excavation. We find a reiteration of the narrative of subjectification, but one that is continually exposed as false. This is not an encounter with the other so much as it is the realization that the creation of subjects, in and of itself, is oppressive, painful and perverse. The affection-image, when it is mobilized towards its most radical potential, provokes us to both feel and think this fact.

Chapter 6

Schizoanalysis, Spectacle and the Spaghetti Western

David Martin-Jones

This chapter uses the notion of the cinematic spectacle to explore some of the potential benefits and limitations of a schizoanalysis of cinema. The argument is illustrated using one of the most famous spaghetti westerns of all time, Sergio Corbucci's *Django* (1966). Initially the chapter examines the growing importance of the role of spectacle in academic writing on cinema, culminating in a brief introduction to the two most relevant works for this chapter: Rosie Thomas's seminal piece on popular Indian cinema (1985), and Tom Gunning's influential reconsideration of early silent cinema (1989). In light of these developments, focusing on recent reconsiderations of the spaghetti western the chapter illustrates how a greater, contextualized understanding of the mode of production and consumption of the cinematic spectacle can inform discussions of a schizoanalysis of cinema. It will be seen that, as all films belong to a complex assemblage, of industry, aesthetic, context and reception, a multi-faceted schizoanalysis of cinema depends on a number of external factors beyond the purely formal.

Deleuze, cinema, schizoanalysis

Formally, Deleuze's two major image categories of the movement-image and the time-image can be understood as manifestations of cinema in more or less reterritorialized and deterritorialized forms. As I have argued elsewhere, this conception of cinema has its origins in Deleuze and Félix Guattari's analysis of the interactive interplay between different planes of immanence in *A Thousand Plateaus* (1980) (Martin-Jones, 2006: 25–7). The movement-image can be seen to exist on what Deleuze and Guattari referred to as the reterritorialized 'plane of organization', while the time-image emerges on its interactive partner, the deterritorializing 'plane of consistency' (270). Like these two interactive planes, the movement-image and the time-image are caught up in the struggle between the reterritorializing powers of the movement-image, and its deterritorializing partner, the time-image. The interplay between the two images enables the perpetual recreation of a self-sustaining impulse. The dominant movement-image is constantly 'threatened' by the potentially destabilizing power of the time-image, but is ultimately able to reimpose itself. This process can be better understood with reference to the cinema books.

In *Cinema 2*, referring to the difference between movement- and time-image cinemas, and the role of montage in constructing these respectively indirect and direct images of time, Deleuze notes that:

> It took the modern cinema to re-read the whole of cinema as already made up of aberrant movements and false continuity shots. The direct time-image is the phantom which has always haunted the cinema, but it took modern cinema to give a body to this phantom. This image is virtual, in opposition to the actuality of the movement-image. (1989: 41)

Modern cinema sees the emergence of the deterritorializing 'phantom' of the time-image, the virtual correlative of the reterritorialized, actual movement-image. Thus, the time-image unlocked the sensory-motor continuity of the movement-image that foregrounded organic link – often represented through the logical progression of character action – which served to spatialize the passing of time in classical cinema. As opposed to the goal-oriented 'doers' of the movement-image, Deleuze considered the protagonist of modern cinema an aimlessly wandering 'seer'. Accordingly, rather than the development of the narrative through the protagonist's action, from situation, through action, to changed situation, (SAS) Deleuze observed in the time-image a temporal hiatus emerging between perception and action. In contrast to the movement-image, the time-image is marked by 'aberrant movements and false continuity shots'. In the time-image the movement of world constructed by montage drives the narrative virtually through time rather than character movement actualizing space-time, as it does in the movement-image.

It is the dynamic de- and reterritorializing interaction of the movement-image and the time-image that provides the conditions for a schizoanalysis of cinema. Yet in his two cinema books Deleuze did not explicitly demonstrate the interconnectedness of the two images in any detail, describing them as image types that seemingly developed independently of each other. However, following the model of interactive planes of *A Thousand*

Plateaus, if we conceive of them as interconnected, as extremes or poles between which individual films flux, then it becomes apparent that a schizoanalysis of cinema – rather than simply categorizing films as either movement- or time-images – can reveal the inherent potential for de- and reterritorializations of cinema into various different image types.

This approach places Deleuze's work on cinema within the larger project of schizoanalysis. Summarizing Deleuze and Guattari's conception of schizoanalysis in *Anti-Oedipus* (1972), Eugene W. Holland notes that:

> The . . . positive task of schizoanalysis is to locate desiring-machines beneath or behind the systems of representation that capture and crush them, and to restore them to their proper molecular functioning. . . . The aim, in short, is to release molecular desire from the constraints of molar representation. (1999: 99)

Correspondingly, the time-image is the product or expression of a desiring-machine with the potential to destabilize the molar, Oedipal reterritorializations of dominant movement-image cinemas like the action-image. Deleuze's twin cinema texts, then, can be seen to function as a schizoanalysis of cinema that champions the time-image for its deterritorializing potential.

Approaching Deleuze's work in this way helps explain the otherwise unusual convergence of these two image types in much contemporary cinema (Pisters, 2003; Martin-Jones, 2006) as evidence of the continued play of de- and reterritorializations of capitalism in its perpetual struggle between molar forms and molecular desire. In *Deleuze and Guattari* (1989), Ronald Bogue describes the functioning of capitalism, stating: 'Capitalism, in its deterritorializing guise, then, sets adrift schizophrenic fluxes of bits and scraps of things, peoples, words, customs and beliefs, which it then reterritorializes in the neurotic Oedipal triangle of papa-mummy-me' (1989: 88–9). Similarly, in cinema, the aberrant narrative time of the time-image deterritorializes the otherwise linear narrative time of the movement-image, setting its wandering seer protagonists adrift in a temporal no-man's land to explore the 'schizophrenic fluxes' opened up by discontinuous temporality, which the movement-image otherwise reterritorializes through continuity editing. Thus, as with the functioning of capitalism, despite the dominance of the reterritorialized form (the movement-image), cinema always retains the deterritorializing potential of the time-image. In contemporary films with aspects of both images, the fluxing of different films between these two poles becomes much clearer.

For a schizoanalysis of cinema to develop, then, it needs to free itself of certain aspects of Deleuze's cinema books. Deleuze's rather static conceptualization of cinema into two image categories is based on an opposition that structures his thinking. In spite of the appearance of several European movement-image cinemas, by the close of *Cinema 1* the dominant form of the movement-image, the action-image, is equated with classical Hollywood cinema. Then, in *Cinema 2* the time-image is directly linked to post-war European art cinema, that of the various new waves. Aside from prematurely fixing the two images into static poses, the difficulty that Deleuze's approach creates is that any number of European popular genres (not to mention numerous national cinemas from Asia and elsewhere), fall into the cracks between these two poles. In his distinction between movement- and time-image, Deleuze demonstrates a rather elitist, Eurocentric position – similar to predecessors like Theodor W. Adorno and Max Horkheimer of the Frankfurt School – that posits Hollywood as the negative counterfoil to a supposedly more critical or advanced European art cinema. Yet, beyond the purely formal conceptualization of cinema offered by Deleuze, films are products of specific industrial conditions, aesthetic traditions, historical contexts, and interact differently with national and international audiences. Accordingly, films which may appear deterritorializing in intent when viewed formally, or in relation to a perceived aesthetic norm like Hollywood, may seem reterritorialized when these contextual factors are considered. Thus, we should not only consider Deleuze's image categories to exist in a complex, fluid interaction, but also acknowledge that the interplay between narrative and spectacle that causes a film to flux between the two extreme poles of the movement- and the time-image is also a product of a specific historical context. In addition to the formal reconsideration of Deleuze's position in the cinema texts that is offered by a schizoanalysis of cinema, then, historically contextualizing cinema necessitates a rethinking of Deleuze's position, here in relation to popular Indian film, early silent cinema and the spaghetti western.

Narrative, spectacle, schizoanalysis

Of most relevance to this discussion of the cinematic spectacle are two pieces that emerged in the 1980s, almost contemporaneous with Deleuze's cinema books. In 'Indian cinema: pleasures and popularity' (1985), Rosie Thomas emphasized that popular Indian cinema (sometimes referred to as Bollywood cinema) was not simply a bad copy of the classical Hollywood form. Such negative assumptions are a product of the unconscious criteria that structure much European and Anglo-American appreciation of cinema. Rather, the narrative of popular Indian cinema is derived from non-Aristotelian aesthetic traditions specific to India, including the epic religious texts the *Ramayana* and the *Mahabharat*, and indigenous theatrical forms drawn from classical, folk and Parsi traditions. The distinctive narrative of popular Indian cinema – with its periodic interruptions for song and dance routines, fight scenes, comedic routines and so on – is a '"ridiculous" pretext for spectacle and emotion' (Thomas, 1985: 123). In popular Indian cinema spectacle is not an interruption of the narrative's linear development. Rather, it is of primary importance in the construction of a constantly shifting 'narrative' of spectacles.

Thomas emphasized that understanding the manner of production and consumption of different cinemas enabled a greater appreciation of film form. In the case of popular Indian cinema, the mode of production is extremely different to that of either the Hollywood studio system or the state supported national cinemas of Europe. The Indian film industry relies on independent venture capital to produce inexpensive films aimed at mass audiences. These audiences expect a film that blends together different moods, generally including several song and dance numbers with which they can participate. Viewers may return to the cinema to see a popular film several times, not because of its innovative narrative, but for the spectacles and the blend of moods they create. Popular Indian films, then, are products of specific market and viewing conditions, and these various contextual factors go a long way towards explaining the specific aesthetic construction of popular Indian cinema.

In terms of a schizoanalysis of cinema, Thomas's work demonstrates that contextual knowledge of cinemas outside of Hollywood and Europe had a direct impact on the extent to which we consider these cinemas to be de- or reterritorializing. The danger that this brief sketch of Thomas's position illuminates is that, if we follow Deleuze's position – an ahistorically considered Hollywood norm (the movement-image) and its European counterpart (the time-image) – then a schizoanalysis of cinema which focuses solely on formal structure may misplace the importance of the historical context in which 'other' cinemas emerge. If popular Indian cinema is not simply a poor copy of the Hollywood movement-image, then to assess the degree to which it de- and reterritorializes the Hollywood product requires a knowledge of the Indian context in which its unique blend of narrative and spectacle emerged.

Similarly, potential problems for a schizoanalysis of cinema pursued in purely formal terms are foregrounded by consideration of Tom Gunning's 'Cinema of attractions: early film, its spectator and the avant-garde' (1989).

Gunning's article covered early silent cinema from approximately 1895–1906, and rethought previous histories of cinema that had, until then, been 'written and theorized under the hegemony of narrative films' (56). Prior to Gunning, histories of cinema had positioned early silent films as the 'primitive' forerunners of a more 'developed' narrative cinema. By contrast, Gunning argued that early silent films were not intended as narratives at all, but were manufactured as attractions to be consumed in the context of vaudeville programmes, where a film was simply one more entertainment on a varied bill. At that time just seeing a film (or indeed, seeing the phenomenon of film) was an attraction in itself. For this reason early silent films should not be understood as primitive attempts at narrative, but as deliberately eye-catching spectacles designed for an audience desirous of immediate distraction. This contextual knowledge explains why many early silent films worked hard to solicit the gaze of the spectator through the use of special effects (slow motion, multiple exposure, etc.), slapstick and other visual gags, direct address to the camera (characters winking at the audience, magicians bowing), the use of close-ups either for titillation, or simply to demonstrate the ability of the new medium to render objects larger than life and so on.

Gunning's intervention drew together two very different cinematic styles, those of the Lumière brothers and Georges Méliès. These early cinema pioneers had previously been considered the forerunners of different film traditions, the non-narrative and narrative respectively. For Gunning, however, they were both part of the cinema of attractions. The early actuality films of the Lumière brothers (where the attraction was a glimpse of real life captured on film, such as workers leaving a factory) were repositioned alongside the trick films of Georges Méliès. For Gunning, in neither instance was there any attempt to create a coherent narrative, as would later emerge in the cinema of directors like D. W. Griffith. Rather, alongside the mundane events captured by the Lumières, any narrative that emerged in the works of Méliès was reconsidered by Gunning as an excuse for a string of otherwise disconnected spectacles. Thus, rather like popular Indian cinema, in early silent cinema, narrative, if there is one at all, is of less importance than the spectacles it enables.

Gunning's criticism of previous evolutionary histories of cinema again illustrates the potential difficulty for a schizoanalysis of cinema posed by Deleuze's formally conceived image categories. To quote Gunning in full:

The history of early cinema, like the history of cinema generally, has been written and theorised under the hegeomony of narrative films.

Early filmmakers, like Smith, Méliès and Porter have been studied primarily from the viewpoint of their contribution to film as a storytelling medium, particularly the evolution of narrative editing. (56)

Although Deleuze was at pains to disavow that his cinema books constructed a history of cinema (1986: xiv), due to the influence of André Bazin (Deleuze's work closely follows the theoretical parameters of *Cahiers du cinéma*), it is clear from the start of *Cinema 1* that in terms of montage Deleuze also sees cinema as an evolutionary art form.

In *Cinema 1*, Deleuze sets out to question Henri Bergson's contention in *Creative Evolution* that cinema could not render visible duration, but only false movement, 'immobile sections + abstract time' (1986: 1). Deleuze argued that, due to the nascent development of cinema when Bergson published his book, it was not possible for him to fully comprehend cinema's potential to create images of time. Providing a brief history of the development of cinema in terms of its ability to present movement and time, Deleuze argued that, contrary to Bergson's position, cinema is able to provide images of duration. This is the case whether it is a movement-image (an indirect image) or a time-image (a direct image). To do so, however, it must reach a certain stage in its evolution that was signified by the appearance of montage.

> The evolution of the cinema, the conquest of its own essence or novelty, was to take place through montage, the mobile camera and the emancipation of the view point, which became separate from projection. The shot would then stop being a spatial category and become a temporal one, and the section would no longer be immobile, but mobile. The camera would rediscover that very movement-image of the first chapter of *Matter and Memory*. (Deleuze, 1986: 3)

Deleuze refers to the static camera that characterized so much early silent cinema as 'a primitive state of the cinema' (1986: 24) due to its inability to capture the (Bazinian) 'essence' of cinema, that which later emerged in the movement- and time-image. These images would only emerge with a mobile camera and montage, which 'intervened to realize a potential contained in the fixed primitive image' (25). Admittedly, Deleuze is not precisely recreating the histories of cinema that positioned early silent film as the primitive form of later narrative cinemas. However, by decontextualizing early silent cinema he does recreate the stance of film historians prior to Gunning, of seeing the cinema of attractions as a primitive form of cinema, rather than a contextually fit-for-purpose mode of film production.

Thus, the point to retain in any discussion of schizoanalysis is that by examining the formal qualities of films in isolation from the contexts in which they operate, it becomes extremely difficult to tell what is a de- and what a reterritorialized form of cinema. Instead we too easily fall into the same trap as Deleuze, of seeing films as belonging to fixed image categories. As the above examples demonstrate, it would be a mistake to consider the purposefully designed stand-alone spectacles of the early silent cinema of attractions as 'primitive' reterritorializations of cinema in relation to the different forms of movement-images that followed the introductions of a mobile camera and montage. Such an approach provides little room for a multi-dimensional schizoanalysis of cinema.

Nowadays film history is no longer considered to be straightforwardly evolutionary as Deleuze's analysis suggests. Instead, perhaps a little ironically considering Deleuze's closeness to Foucault, it is examined as a series of archaeological layers. These layers are context specific, for instance early silent cinema is seen to develop differently in France than it did in India, Iran or Japan. Any effective schizoanalysis of cinema, then, must ensure that different cinematic narratives and spectacles are examined as products of the contexts from which they emerged. From this perspective an informed, multifaceted schizoanalysis of cinema is possible. To demonstrate this more fully I now focus on the spaghetti western, one illustrative example of how understanding the context in which films emerge can facilitate a schizoanalysis of cinema.

Spaghettis, contexts, schizoanalysis

Although usually associated with Italy, the spaghetti western was actually an international co-production genre formula that flourished during the 1960s and 1970s, when over four hundred spaghetti westerns were made (Wagstaff, 1998). Spaghettis were not only popular with audiences in Europe, but also in various parts of South America, the Middle East and Asia. For many years the spaghetti western was misunderstood as a 'primitive' or 'derivative' take on the US western, hence the derogatory nickname. Serious study of the spaghetti western only began to grow with the turn to European popular genre cinema in the early 1990s initiated by Richard Dyer and Ginette Vincendeau's *Popular European Cinema* (1992). Moving beyond initial attempts by Christopher Frayling (1981) to recuperate certain Italian westerns, such as those of Sergio Leone, as 'critical' westerns that formally responded to the ideology of the US form (1981: xxiii), Christopher Wagstaff (1992) and Dimitris Eleftheriotis (2001) turned their attention to the cheaper, and often more widespread serial films, like the Django and Ringo movies, studying them as products of specific contexts. These lower budget serial films greatly outnumber the classical narratives of Leone's westerns. They are also distinctive in their narrative structures, which eschew the psychological motivation and linear development of both US westerns and Leone's films, being marked instead by a repetitious series of spectacles, typically involving gunfights, barroom brawls and other action sequences.

The contextualizing factors foregrounded by these critics enhance our understanding of the extent to which spaghettis de- and reterritorialize the western format, which was, at that time, dominated by the Hollywood genre model. Like both early silent and popular Indian cinema, a schizoanalysis of the spaghetti western relies as much on the extent to which it can be seen to be fit for purpose, as it does on formal comparison with a dominant, apparently normative US movement-image. In this way a contextually informed schizoanalysis of cinema avoids positioning spaghettis as simply a poorly de- or reterritorialized version of the Hollywood movement-image, enabling a greater appreciation of the degrees to which it both de- and reterritorializes the genre for context-specific ends.

For Deleuze the US western genre was a typical example of the action-image (the dominant form of the movement-image), providing the 'purest state' (1986: 153) of the duel that marked the linear movement from situation through action (the duel) to changed situation (SAS). It would be extremely tempting, then, to deploy Frayling's argument from Leone's films to suggest that certain spaghettis effectively deterritorialize the ideology of the US western with a purposefully overblown, almost Brechtian style, which foregrounds and parodies the norms of the genre. Yet as Wagstaff notes, while Frayling's approach enabled him to intellectually reclaim the Leone westerns, it does not work for movies like *Django* (260). Viewed formally, the episodic string of spectacles that constitute the narrative of spaghettis like *Django* could be considered a de- or reterritorialization of the linear movement of the narrative of the US western. Rather than the SAS structure of the US western, the structure of spaghettis like *Django* might perhaps be rendered SSSSS . . . The decision as to whether this constitutes a de- or reterritorialization of the US western would then depend on the analyst's approach to the form of the chosen film or films. On the other hand, if we schizoanalyse the spaghetti western by examining its historically defining contexts of production and consumption, then its episodic, spectacular structure can be seen to at once de- *and* reterritorialize the schizo desires underlying the US western when it is reproduced and consumed in its spaghetti format.

Analysing the spaghetti western specifically within the Italian national context, Wagstaff provides a detailed account both of the industrial factors relating to their production context, and of the manner in which they were consumed. Industrially, the spaghetti western was a result of a number of conditions, including a fragmented production sector made up of numerous small companies, the limited possibilities for distribution and the consequently conservative approach of distributors, and the available state subsidies and tax rebates favouring international co-productions. Together these factors were conducive to the production of serial low budget genre films that, due to the specifics of this situation, practically guaranteed producers a return on their money (1992: 249–51). Thus spaghettis flourished alongside a number of other popular genres, including the *peplum* (epic hero-fantasy films), *giallo* (detective stories), historical epics, comedies, adventures, melodramas, sex films, horror films and so on.

Wagstaff focuses on the reception of the cheaply made '*terza visione*' (third run) spaghetti westerns, which ran in outlying areas of Italy and were more numerous than the urban-based '*prima*' and '*seconda visione*' (first and second run) westerns.

> The audience of the *terza visione* cinema was more like the television audience than like a *prima visione* cinema audience. The viewer (generally he) went to the cinema nearest to his house (or in rural areas, the only cinema there was) after dinner, at around ten o'clock in the evening. The programme changed daily or every other day. He would not bother to find out what was showing, nor would he make any particular effort to arrive at the beginning of the film. He would talk to his friends during the showing whenever he felt like it, except during the bits of the film that grabs his (or his friends') attention. . . . People would be coming and going and changing seats throughout the performance. (1992: 253)

In such viewing conditions, Wagstaff notes, the episodic narrative of spaghettis makes perfect sense. A series of spectacles, offering either 'laughter, thrills [or] titillation' (253) acted rather like a cinema of attractions to hail or court the constantly wandering attention of its viewers. For this reason the psychological realism of the US western, or of a *prima visione* western like those of Leone, is missing from the spaghetti western. Its episodic structure is a radical deterritorialization of the SAS narrative of the classical Hollywood western into a series of markers of the genre (gun fights, bar-room punch-ups, horseback rides, abductions of prostitutes, massa-cring of settlers, etc.). These markers are then re-territorialized into a string of spectacles designed to target a specific audience's viewing patterns. As a result these films remain movement-images, but there is far less con-nection between situation and action than in the action-image. Characters do not become equal to their situation through action as they do in an action-image. Rather, actions take place in situations which – to use the old western maxim – just 'happen along' in an SSSSS . . . pattern. In this respect spaghettis formally veer towards the pole of the time-image in order to meet their audience's needs. The actions of the characters are equal to those changing situations, but they do not cause them to change as they do in the US western.

The narrative trajectory of *Django* is extremely straightforward. Django (Franco Nero) arrives in town looking for revenge, kills practically everyone, the end. It is not the narrative, then, that is the point of the film, but the spectacles that it enables. Django is involved in, or witness to, a number of scenes which serve no narrative purpose. These include: the prolonged whipping of a whore; the shooting of several of General Hugo's (Jose Bodalo) bandits; Django killing several of Major Jackson's (Eduardo Fajardo) men; Major Jackson and his henchman Ringo sadisti-cally shooting Mexican peasant-farmers as they run for their lives; Django shooting more of Major Jackson's men in a bar; Django shooting yet more of Major Jackson's men with a big machine gun; three whores mud wrestling; Hugo and his bandits cutting off the ear of a corrupt priest and feeding it to him; a machine gun ambush of a military fort; the robbery of the fort's gold; a horse chase that ends at the border; a bar-room fist fight; a strip tease, the machine gunning of Hugo's men; the crippling of Django's hands by rifle butt and horses' hooves; an ambush in which Major Jackson's men kill General Hugo and his men; and a final shoot out in a cemetery in which Django kills Major Jackson.

Through these various spectacles Django walks, dragging behind him the coffin containing his machine gun. His actions in these situations do not change them for the better. Rather, the spaghetti's narrative facilitates a series of spectacles or attractions, focusing on Django's superhuman ability to act, and especially to shoot. The spaghetti western's SSSSS . . . pattern pro-vides a direct equivalence between character movement (the unifying drive of the movement-image) and the movement of world (Deleuze, 1989: 61) we find in the discontinuous editing of the time-image. It is as though in the series of spectacles of the spaghetti western the movement-image and the time-image run parallel to each other. Character action is equal to each new situation (as in the movement-image), but action cannot drive the narrative alone, and a discontinuous movement of montage from situation to situation also takes place (as in the time-image). With Wagstaff's position in mind, then, it would seem appropriate for a schizoanalysis of the spaghetti western to consider this genre both a de- *and* a reterritorialization of the US western. The classical narrative drive of the US genre is deterritorialized. Its exploration of character motivation, and the interaction between character and milieu of the SAS format are refigured, reconstituted as disconnected spectacles. On the other hand, it is reterritorialized into a format that suits the context-specific ends to which these films were designed, the distribution context and the audience viewing conditions of the *terza visione* cinemas of Italy in the 1960s and 1970s. Thus Wagstaff's nationally contextualizing position on spaghettis illustrates that their reterritorializing aspect is much stronger than a purely formal comparison which the US western might suggest. A schizoanalysis of the spaghetti western from a perspective informed by Wagstaff might conclude that while it is formally deterritorialized in comparison to the US western, it is reterritorialized within its national context of production and reception.

Even so, Wagstaff's position is not the only available context from which to draw a schizoanalysis of the spaghetti western. In *Popular Cinemas of Europe* (2001) Dimitris Eleftheriotis developed the debate surrounding the spaghetti western in a broader international arena. Although popular with Italian audiences, spaghettis were constructed to appeal beyond national boundaries, often produced with finance from some combination of Italy, Spain, France and Germany and then dubbed and exported to various destinations across Europe the Middle East, South America and Asia. From this broader contextual position, Eleftheriotis argued that spaghetti westerns should be understood as providing viewers in the 1960s and 1970s Europe, South America, the Middle East and Asia with a form of 'fantasy tourism' or 'pauper's travelling' (128) in which they journeyed into a fantastic version of the old west, and took part in a series of spectacles recognizable from US westerns. In a context of increased US global dominance, the spaghetti western provided audiences worldwide with a chance to reciprocate the movements of the various flows of people and money (from tourism to commerce to military intervention) emanating from the United States. This complex process of 'transculturation' – a term which Eleftheriotis borrows from Mary Louise Pratt's work on travel writing – ensures that spaghettis remain westerns, but are simultaneously transformed into a spaghetti guise. As he argues: 'The American genre functions as raw material, which after its transformation in the process of production, is delivered to national and international markets, usually (but not always) disguised as American' (103). When viewed in this light the spaghetti western again appears to be both a deterritorialization of the US western, and simultaneously a reterritorialization of the genre into a new form. This time, however, it is seen to transform for rather different reasons (the enabling of virtual tourism for global audiences), which explain the genre's popularity in many parts of the world.

Again the role of spectacle is integral to this process. Eleftheriotis comments at length on how Django's individualism detaches him from the contexts in which he acts, contexts which are reduced to mere backgrounds to his actions. He notes in addition the purely spectacular functioning of the absurd sight of Django slowly lugging his coffin everywhere on foot, the red Ku Klux Klan style hoods of Major Jackson's men that stand out against the drab and muddy town, and so on (123–4). This spectacular recreation of the old west ensures the international accessibility of the spaghetti western as a fantastical travel genre, by deliberately erasing the normally defining national identity of characters in the US genre (126–7). Eleftheriotis concludes his analysis by stating that, aiming at an international market, spaghettis shatter

> [T]he particular relationship between historical events, ideological operations, cultural meanings and aesthetic forms that defines the American genre. . . . [T]his involves first a weakening of the historical referent by structuring the film around the presence of unique heroes who transcend historical and cultural specificity; second, a disengagement of the *mise-en-scène* from the ideological and iconographic values of the American western; and finally, a detachment of the heroes from a point of view system that could place them in an interactive relationship with other characters. (124)

The international context in which these films circulated, then, provides yet another perspective on their form, and in particular their construction and deployment of cinematic spectacle as an end in itself. In contrast to Wagstaff's nationally contextualizing direction, a schizoanalysis of the spaghetti western from a perspective informed by Eleftheriotis's position would conclude that as a genre it is far more deterritorialized than reterritorialized. Its international aim led to the deliberate construction of an identity-less arrangement of spectacles that would appeal universally. The only common factor for all viewers, be they Italian or in any other country peripheral to the United States but subject to its influence, is the fantasy tourism (and corresponding pleasure of a virtual invasion of the US genre) enabled by the detaching of the hero from his context. As was the case in Wagstaff's argument, in Deleuzian terms the spaghetti ensures the replacement of the SAS pattern in which the doer's role is vital to narrative progression with the parallel movements of character actions and various situations (of movement- and time-image). This time, however, due to the larger scope of the context, this deterritorialization appears much more influential than the reterritorializing force seen by Wagstaff to be reshaping the spaghetti western for Italian audiences, a conclusion reached when we appreciate the genre's need to appeal to international audiences.

In conclusion, then, analysing the context-specific ends to which different types of cinematic spectacles have been produced illustrates the need for a contextual understanding of cinema if a truly multi-dimensional schizoanalysis is to be undertaken.

Chapter 7

Cinemas of Minor Frenchness

Bill Marshall

In the first few years of the twenty-first century, the cinema of Quebec has been on somewhat of a roll, with its share of the domestic box-office reaching double figures in percentage terms, and a few breakthrough films enjoying success on the international art-house circuit: *Les Invasions barbares/The Barbarian Invasions* (dir. Denys Arcand, 2003; recipient of the Oscar for best foreign language film in 2004); *La Grande Séduction/Seducing Doctor Lewis* (dir. Jean-François Pouliot, 2003); *C.R.A.Z.Y.* (dir. Jean-Marc Vallée, 2005).[1] Quebec cinema operates within a peculiar cultural and political context, with a – to an extent – unresolved national question (the failed sovereignty referenda of 1980 and 1995), and a minority, peripheral status in relation both to anglophone Canada and the rest of North America, and to the language and culture of metropolitan France.

In *Cinema 2: The Time-Image*, Gilles Deleuze famously analysed the work of one Quebec documentary filmmaker working in the 1960s, Pierre Perrault. In the latter's *Pour la suite du monde* (1963), for example, the filmmakers encourage the re-enactment of a traditional method of hunting beluga whale on an island in the St Lawrence, and overcome some of the dilemmas of ethnographic cinema and its subject-object relations. The peoples of the island are 'intercessors' because they are real but engaged in creating fictions and legends, and a reciprocal communication and transformation characterize their relationship with the filmmakers. Time is the force that here puts truth in crisis. Through fabulation, Perrault and his cameraman Michel Brault are freed from a model of truth, and what Deleuze, drawing on Nietzsche, calls the 'power of the false' breaks the repetition of the past and provokes, not a recalling, but a calling forth. As with the (other) Third World filmmakers he examines, such as Ousmane Sembene and Glauber Rocha, Deleuze sees *Pour la suite du monde* as an example of 'minor' cinema in which 'the people' are perceived as 'lacking' rather than offering a full identity or presence:

> What cinema must grasp is not the identity of a character, whether real *or* fictional, through his objective and subjective aspects. It is the becoming

of the real character when he himself starts to 'make fiction', when he enters into 'the flagrant offence of making up legends' and so contributes to the invention of his people. The character is inseparable from a before and an after, but he reunites these in the passage from one state to the other. He himself becomes another, when he begins to tell stories without ever being fictional. And the film-maker for his part becomes another when there are 'interposed', in this way, real characters who wholly replace his own fictions by his own story-telling. (Deleuze, 1989: 150)

However, the potential for Deleuzian thought to address the situation of Quebec does not end here in the pages of *The Time-Image*. Explicitly in the 'Postulates on Linguistics' section of *A Thousand Plateaus,* and implicitly in their work on Kafka and even the anti-Oedipal positions elaborated elsewhere in their collaboration, Deleuze and Guattari begin to suggest what a 'minor' Frenchness might be.

In their ontology of becoming rather than being, of movement, process and multiplicity rather than fixity and identity, and in their sidestepping of the binaries of self/other and subject/object, Deleuze and Guattari emphasize the fact that the 'proper name' ('the instantaneous apprehension of a multiplicity' (Deleuze and Guattari, 1987: 37)), as in 'Québécois', is always already pluralized, its bits, components, particles, molecules, arranged and organized according to bigger, molar, structures, but at the same time potentially taking off in new directions: 'Signs are not signs of a thing; they are signs of deterritorialization and reterritorialization, they mark a certain threshold crossed in the course of these movements' (Deleuze and Guattari, 1987: 67). The Quebec national project is riven with the tension between territorialization and deterritorialization because of the competing discourses of 'Québécité' and 'Américanité', continental and Atlantic identities, the migrant flows of globalized capital into which it is unevenly inserted, the different relationships lived with Canada, and above all the shifting categories of majority and minority. Deleuze and Guattari conceive the 'minor' not in terms of numbers, but in terms of the relationship between becoming and the territorialization/deterritorialization process. The writings of Kafka, or of African-Americans, or of the Irish, all possess an ambiguous relationship to the 'major' language in which they write, which they affect with 'a high coefficient of deterritorialization' (Deleuze and Guattari, 1986: 16). Kafka, for example, wrote German as a Jew excluded from the German-speaking minority in a peripheral city of an empire in which German was a commercial lingua franca but was not 'at home'. Quebec artists of the 1960s, to take another example, were conscious that their language was 'minor' in relation not only to the vast North American and Canadian anglophone majority, but was peripheral and relatively deterritorialized faced with the 'major' language that is standard metropolitan French. This implies, as when Fredric Jameson (1986), drawing on Deleuze and Guattari's work, writes of national allegory, that any individual utterance is always already in this context magnified to embrace politically the whole collectivity. Indeed, for Deleuze and Guattari, 'There is no individual enunciation', since enunciation always implies 'collective assemblages' and we all speak in indirect discourse (Deleuze and Guattari, 1987: 79–80). The point is not to talk about Quebec French as a particular dialect, but to realize that 'minor' and 'major' attitudes can be adopted towards this language and culture. One is either to fall back on to a new territorialization: 'the Canadian singer can also bring about the most reactionary, the most Oedipal of reterritorializations, oh mama, oh my native land, my cabin, olé, olé' (Deleuze and Guattari, 1987: 24). Or the other is to follow the logic of the 'minor' status, its capacity for proliferation and innovation (becoming), its antithesis therefore to the rank of master, and its undermining of the 'major' culture's pretensions to the natural, normal and universal: 'It is a question not of reterritorializing oneself on a dialect or patois but of deterritorializing the major language' (Deleuze and Guattari, 1987: 104). Minorities both have their own territorialities but must also be considered as 'seeds, crystals of becoming whose value is to trigger uncontrollable movements and deterritorializations of the mean or majority' (Deleuze and Guattari, 1987: 134). The 'minor' languages and cultures that emerge may be completely innovative. In this context, the 'national allegory' is best described as a 'national-allegorical tension' between these centripetal and centrifugal forces (Marshall, 2001).

Deleuze's canon of films (articulated in his cinema books) is open to some question; for example, he tended to select one film director from a 'third-world' country, usually the one taken up by *Cahiers du cinéma*, hence his choice of Perrault. He might instead have alighted upon *A tout prendre*, a little-known gem of world cinema, shot in 1961–3 and released in 1964, which revels in 'the minor', but, paradoxically, a minor mode constructed from within the urban bourgeoisie (and whose main protagonist speaks impeccable metropolitan French). This quasi-autobiographical piece, produced in the private sector, portrays the affair between filmmaker Claude (Claude Jutra), and a Black model, Johanne (Johanne Harel), who is still living with her (estranged and unseen) husband. The vicissitudes of the relationship – first encounter, obsession, other dalliances, Johanne's pregnancy, subsequent rejection by Claude, and miscarriage – are less important than the way the film combines the formal experimentation of its *cinematic* language with a sustained problematization of identity itself. *A tout prendre* joyously undercuts the 'self' on which the film would seem narcissistically to centre. From the opening scene in which Claude gets ready for the party, the spectator is confronted with the fragility of the 'self'. The 'realism' of body details in the shower (such as washing feet) combines with a montage of shots of Claude in various guises in front of the mirror, ending with him firing a gun so that it shatters and fragments. The self-proclaimed 'quest' of the film is to 'get rid of my youth and of the characters [*personnages*] inside me'. The film proceeds to address this longing, but ultimately Claude discovers that there is no unified identity for him to step into. Claude and Johanne circle each other in the photography scene not in some closed repetition but in a relationship of mutual dependency and attraction: they consist of bits, fragments, atoms, rather than complete and finished persons or identities (although Johanne ultimately turns out to be trapped within the desire for wholeness predicated on heterosexual romance). In fact, 'Je est un autre', 'I is another' (the quotation from Rimbaud's *Lettre du voyant* of 1871 which Deleuze uses to describe the non-identical in time and the non-identity of image and concept, and which he sees manifesting itself in Jean Rouch's practice in *Moi, un noir*). The way forward is through fabulation.

    Crucially, and this is where it leaves far behind the world of *Pour la suite du monde*, *A tout prendre* is also about sex and its relation to identity (or non-identity). The gaze of Claude upon Johanne is not to be characterized as the standard male heterosexual gaze of mainstream Hollywood and even art cinema, fixing the threatening female body as an object of voyeurism or fetishism. Claude's position is continuously undermined by what we might term the apprenticeship of difference that Johanne forces him to experience. This is the case in terms of race (she explicitly refuses to be exoticized), her own identity masquerade, in the troubling scenes when Claude's gaze is returned (notably by Johanne and Barbara [Monique Mercure]), and most notably in the acknowledgement of his own homosexual inclinations that she in fact provokes. Claude's 'identity' or rather *plurality* of identities, is thus predicated on a dialogue with otherness, a becoming-other. The lessons for Quebec are that any national struggle must be predicated on provisional and not full or unified notions of identity. The fact that *A tout prendre* can be co-opted only with considerable difficulty for a political project extends also to identity politics. The refreshing – and astonishing for 1963 – treatment of homosexuality is far from constituting an 'identity' (Johanne's phrase, 'do you like boys?', is based on *acts*).

It prompts Claude to *act*, by, it is heavily implied, seducing the lead actor of his film, but the fact that gay assertion goes no further is attributable not only to the historical context. The film cannot be read as a straightforward assertion of 'Quebec' either. Its treatment of its identity position(s) is decidedly, and triumphantly, 'minor'.

This is the point missed by contemporary commentators such as Denys Arcand, who identified national maturity with heterosexual relations with one's own', 'women of the real, of the everyday': 'There we find, I think, an unconscious refusal to coincide with one's collective self' (Arcand, 1964: 96). For the dominant sexual hermeneutic in Quebec national cinema at the time, and even afterwards, was relentlessly Oedipal. A 1964 article by the editor of the nationalist intellectual journal *Parti pris*, Pierre Maheu, arguing against the compensatory myths articulated by the 'false fathers' or 'pères en jupe/fathers in skirts' of the Catholic Church illustrates this point. In its place he seeks a subjectivity which seriously seeks to tackle the legacy of Quebec's 'colonial Oedipus' (Maheu, 1964) that subjectivity purports to be a universal-national one, but in fact it is profoundly gendered and heterosexualized. Instead of a failed and castrated 'virility' which is afraid to speak its name and to act, Maheu seeks a new paternal position, what Robert Schwartzwald has termed a 'phallo-national maturity' (Schwartzwald, 1991: 181):

> The world of the father is the universe of *hard* objects, of objectal reality, of concrete achievements, of work and efficiency; the Father is praxis, and our myth sentenced us to *sterile* projections. (Maheu, 1964: 24)

It is a world in which there was an 'absence of vital energy and sense of adventure' (Maheu, 1964: 26 my emphasis). For Maheu, Quebec man is Oedipus because he marries his mother, who is herself 'abandoned to frigidity' because she castrates her sons and husband, refusing them 'any *authentic* encounter with masculinity' (my emphasis). Against this phallo-national maturity, this plenitude of virility associated with the nationalist project, is posited the traditional world based on the cult of the mother eternally fixed and rooted in nature. As a result, all wholeness and plenitude are lost:

> We live in a disintegrated culture, a life reduced to scattered crumbs. We lack the social structures essential for integrating the individual and show him a role to play, diversified, efficient, paternal institutions (. . .) depersonalization is that social mush that threatens to swallow us up in the shifting sands of the Mother. (Maheu, 1964: 27)

Maheu is astute enough to seek to include women in his national project, but it is he believes by resurrecting and transforming the idea of 'la Terre-Mère/Mother-Soil' that the nation as *totality* can be embraced once again. The article is in this sense very much an artefact of its times: in the name of a liberation yet to come, it mistakes its own highly gendered position for a universal one, and suggests (sexual) emancipations for both men and women which are highly one-sided: 'make woman into lover and wife and free us from the Mother by bursting from her breast once more, armed and ready for a new battle'. No longer the colonial Oedipus but very Oedipalized in its proposed 'solution' of the Oedipus complex, in the sense of retaining fixed assignments of gendered subjectivity and male power in the family romance or in genital heterosexuality. The whole scenario is in fact a disavowal of that lack, that tension, at the heart of national or any other identity.

Quebec cinema has abounded in father–son narratives (*Les Invasions barbares* and *C.R.A.Z.Y.,* mentioned above, to name but two). An influential study, Heinz Weinmann's *Cinéma de l'imaginaire québécois* (1990) provided suggestive but heavily Oedipalized readings of film texts from Quebec as allegories of the nation in terms of the Freudian family romance, with 'France', 'Britain', the Catholic Church and the patron St John the Baptist as shifting parental figures within a teleology of national 'maturity'. There are thus two strands in Quebec cinema and in critical positions on that cinema: one which constructs a national position read in unified, masculine, heterosexual and Oedipal terms; and one which is more hetero-geneous, challenging that dominant masculine position, qualifying it by seeking to articulate with it other key terms such as class, or jettisoning unity and the national-Oedipal scenario altogether. Women's cinema in Quebec has on occasions constituted the terrain of the latter interroga-tions, as in the work of Anne-Claire Poirier, and of Mireille Dansereau, whose *La Vie rêvée* (1972) resembles *A tout prendre* in its witty feminization of that film's ludic fragmenting of the self.

I wish however to interrogate these Oedipal and anti-Oedipal strands by looking at two examples of genre cinema: Jean-Claude Lauzon's first feature, *Un Zoo la nuit* of 1987, a *policier* owing its sets, decor and iconogra-phy (notably the villainous police) to Jean-Jacques Beineix's *Diva,* but with very national-Québécois features too; and Yves Simoneau's second feature, *Pouvoir intime* of 1986.

Un Zoo la nuit opens with Marcel (Gilles Maheu) being released from prison after serving a two-year sentence for involvement in a drug scam. The two policemen who set him up now want the money. With the help of

an American former cellmate, the police are killed. Meanwhile, Marcel had renewed contact with his divorced father Albert (Roger Le Bel), whom he takes from his hospital bed on one last hunting trip before he dies, to a zoo where he shoots an elephant.

For Weinmann (1990), the film is proof of the maturing of Québécois identity, in that Marcel is able to recognize his father (it is even suggested that the person of René Lévesque, first nationalist premier of Quebec, was a 'father of the nation', and had contributed in the 1970s and 1980s to the rehabilitation of the figure of the father in Quebec culture). For this to happen, of course, the 'bad father', George (Lorne Brass), the sadistic, crooked, gay and *English-Canadian* policeman, has to be physically eliminated. This occurs when he is lured for sex with the ally from the United States.

However, this masculinist national narrative is in fact full of sexual anxiety. Weinmann misses the point when he writes, 'By eliminating George, he eliminates at the same time his own homosexual drives towards his own father which prevent the expression of their father–son relationship' (Weinmann, 1990: 116). This spectacular disavowal (gay-baiting and murder, 'justified' by the spectacle provided by George's sadism and by the prisoner he sent to rape Marcel in his cell at the start of the film) is necessary to legitimate the extraordinary final scene when Marcel washes Albert's naked body and then climbs, naked himself, into bed with him. As in *Parti pris* writing of the 1960s, the 'feminization' of the conquered Quebec is reversed so that it is the English-Canadian, and the 'fédéraste' pro-Canada Québécois such as Pierre Trudeau, who are tainted with (passive) homosexuality. The terror of anal penetration is rife throughout, as when Julie (Lynn Adams) suggests to Marcel, 'Your club sandwich, you can sit on it'. Notably, Julie, the only woman in the film who is not a mother-figure, is a prostitute, and Marcel's dominance over her is asserted when he first has sex with her after his release, a forced coupling filmed with him standing up.

The film clearly presents the source of these anxieties even as it seeks to disavow them. Robert Schwartzwald argues that the 1960s discourse of decolonization in Quebec eventually opted for the assertion of new whole identities rather than the deconstruction of those fixities handed down from the past. What won out was 'the primacy of a political moment in which the task was to constitute whole Subjects capable of finding a *way out* of the very fragmentation that constitutes the generative moment of postmodernist thought' (Schwartzwald, 1991: 178). *Un Zoo la nuit* thus favours a 'major' rather than 'minor' response to the changed status of women (Albert's wife has left *him*; Julie's defiance is subdued and she can

be inserted into a rescue narrative), but also immigrants and multicultural-
ism, globalization and the relationship in content and form between the
traditional, the modern and the postmodern.

  Albert belongs to the urban working class that emerged from modernity and industrialization. That culture is made to lock seamlessly into more
traditional, that is rural, practices of hunting and fishing (the bonding with
Marcel when he teaches him fishing lore on the lake) to form a national
historical plenitude. (Weinmann (1990: 118), like Lauzon, neglects the fact
that the transmission of that culture from the native peoples to the *voya-
geurs* and *coureurs de bois* is problematic, not a source of plenitude.) Albert,
however, has lost his job to the process of globalization, as his factory
closed and the production process moved to the United States. When
Marcel presents him with a 1957 Buick, he remarks, 'The Japanese wouldn't
have made that', locating him within the certainties of post-war Fordism
(and, by implication, 1950s sexual roles). The Italian community where he
lives, and which Marcel initially seems to embrace as a substitute family, is
also viewed competitively. The restaurant owner Toni has accompanied him
on the hunt, the elephant shoot represents one up on him. Marcel is the
urban artist (musician), living in a loft, defining himself through consumer-
ism and its fractured identities, most notably the consumption of drugs.
The dialogue with Albert takes place at first in the interface of those worlds,
a disembodied message from Albert on Marcel's answering machine that
stresses the contrast of generations and epochs ('I'm your father and you're
my boy. That still means something to me'); Albert hides the drug money
in that metonym of working-class life, his old lunch box.

  Albert thus represents an 'authenticity' under threat, and while the
film does not suggest a return to the 1950s, far from it, it works, primarily
through its Oedipal, homosocial and homophobic narrative, to renew contact with that identity while reworking it for the present. Marcel's pro-
claimed love for his father reaches its apotheosis after he has gone on his
own hunt, the *chasse à pédé* which kills the policemen. That action is itself a
reassertion of his prowess after the momentary defeat when Julie is threatened with death behind the peep-show glass partition. Marcel's active
virility is able symbolically to penetrate that screen, to cross it so that he is
able to impose his own reality on it (the whole film presents a gradual breaking down of barriers, symbolic or otherwise, from the opening in which
Marcel's rape is filmed through prison bars through the partitions demol-
ished at Albert's home to the passage through the enclosures of the zoo).
He is thus able to prove he can actively get beyond mere questions of style,
hedonism and consumption, and correct Albert's assertion that 'You young

people think you've changed the world just because you wear dark glasses at night'. In turn, Albert's last venture is aided by a sniff of cocaine provided by Marcel. Significantly, however, the Oedipal narrative's impetus does not carry Marcel as far as the formation of the heterosexual couple, the classic formulation of the reconciliation of desire and the law of the father.

Moreover, the form or forms of the film belie any linear and totalizing reading. Clearly, what is unusual about *Un Zoo la nuit* is its combination of *policier* violence and family drama. However, that contrast represents two distinct kinds of filmmaking for two distinct world views which explain the federating market success of the film but undermine its professed coherence. Marcel's eventual 'crossing' of the peep-show barrier into his own action is in fact a passage from one film quotation (Wenders' *Paris Texas*, later to be followed by a reference to *The American Friend*) to another (the designer violence of contemporary American mob movies as well as French films such as *Diva* and *Subway*: the violence is explicit but filmed in a highly stylized *mise en scène* of orange light, shadows and corridors at a seedy hotel). In contrast, the scenes with Albert in the milieu of the Italian restaurant, for example, are shot by cinematographer Guy Dufaux according to the dominant Quebec realist style with painterly, rich, Brault-like flourishes for the fishing sequence. The very gendered national 'authenticity' at the heart of the film is thus demonstrably a construction, its neurotic masculinity finally unable fully to fill the lack, to stitch together the unravellings provoked by historical, economic and cultural globalization and the de-traditionalization of identity. Albert's home is literally rebuilt around him, and it is unclear what shape it will metaphorically take following his death.

In contrast, Yves Simoneau's *Pouvoir intime* offers a powerful meditation on gender, sexuality and nation. Written by Simoneau and one of the film's stars, Pierre Curzi, *Pouvoir intime* is basically a heist movie with intimations of the postmodern. Two corrupt officials, chief of police Meurseault (Jean-Louis Millette) and the Ministry of Justice security chief, H. B. (Yvan Ponton), recruit a thief, Théo (Jacques Godin) to steal from a security van containing money but also an incriminating document. Théo in turn recruits his teenage son, Robin (Eric Brisebois), another professional criminal, Gildor (Pierre Curzi), who in turn recruits an ex-lover, Roxanne (Marie Tifo). Their action goes wrong from the start: the guard accomplice absents himself, Robin panics and shoots three guards dead and the team have to drive the still locked van to their hideout and attempt to get the surviving guard Martial (Robert Gravel) to leave it, a struggle that takes up a third of the film. By the end, the conspirators and thieves are all dead except for

Roxanne and Janvier (Jacques Lussier), Martial's gay lover whom Roxane had brought to the hideout in order to put pressure on Martial. They go on their separate ways with some of the loot.

Discussion of the film has made much of the gay element in what seems after all to be a genre movie. Gilles Thérien, in a survey of 1980s films that for him bear the mark of the failed sovereignty-association referendum, argues that it is another example of the way in which homosexuality represents an identity dead end for Quebec. Partly drawing on Jacques Lavigne's work *L'Objectivité* of 1971, Thérien argues that homosexuality involves a failure to engage with the Other. The tragedy of *Pouvoir intime* lies in the collapse of all its relations of alterity: law/not law, male/female, father/son. We are left with the Same, the gay man and the androgynous woman who then separate: 'Real homosexuality, false feminine, victory of the homoethical, horizontal level against the vertical hierarchy of power' (Thérien, 1987: 111). Homosexuality thus summarizes Quebec's intermediary situation, 'in between' the self-isolation of the pre-1960 Duplessis era and the uncertainties of struggle and liberation 'out there' in the world. Once again, Quebec is seen as peculiarly lacking a national father-figure, and this prevents it launching into an Oedipal revolt, 'incapable of reaching the Other as Other, alterity as a heterogeneous social given, and of going back to take up the question of origins, the question of identity' (Thérien, 1987: 113–14).

Suffice it to say here that Thérien presents 'Quebec' and 'homosexuality' as mutually exclusive, his developmental model is highly dubious, and his notions of Same/Other seem to be as lacking in engagement with alterity as the texts he criticizes. There is no logical reason why a homosexual relationship should automatically imply a relationship to the Same rather than between two highly heterogeneous entities marked by a multiplicity of discourses of social position. Thérien's quest for identity through alterity in fact proposes a highly homogenizing mapping of binary oppositions and a master discourse of heterosexuality. As for the film, it provides no evidence that its arrangements are to be considered as anxiety-ridden impasses.[2]

In contrast, Henry Garrity (1989–90) argues that *Pouvoir intime* articulates an effective subversive discourse and valorizes the critique of vertical hierarchies of power. He uses Deleuze and Guattari's *Anti-Oedipus* to analyse the thieves as the agents of a molecular defiance and dispersal of the molar structures of state power. The police are entirely absent apart from a second-long glimpse of vehicles going in the wrong direction, and the sound of sirens. Those most locked in the structures of group or territorialized identity fail, those who 'deterritorialize by refusing predetermined roles'

(Garrity, 1989–90: 34) succeed (including Martial who dies but prevents the principal robbery). The final, heavily symbolic scene as Roxanne and Janvier share the cash in an abandoned and burned out church – a reverse marriage ceremony in the landscape of Quebec's post-Catholicism – represents the final triumph of the individual over the macrostructures.

Although this analysis is certainly on the right lines, the equation of subversion and individualism needs to be questioned. The radical decodings that occur in the film go against any Oedipal, masculinist but also individualist outlook. They involve sexual and gender roles, as well as attitudes to the state, but also the way in which desire is organized in the genre movie. *Pouvoir intime* is in this sense the most radical Quebec film since *A tout prendre*, not simply because of its sympathetic gay characters but because it questions and renders provisional all social identities while at the same time offering an enticing glimpse of possible utopian futures.

The first reason for this is the place of the film within genre cinema. The dominant auteurist strain in Quebec cinema from the establishment of regular production in the early 1970s was accompanied by the attempt to create a 'popular' cinema, but mainly through comedy and a symbiosis with television performers and performances. Unlike, obviously, in Hollywood or even in France, where comedies and *policiers* play an important role in the film industry, genre remains a marginal activity within Quebec production. It is therefore interesting to see the reworkings to which a Quebec genre film is submitted. *Pouvoir intime* refuses the pleasures and identifications of the Hollywood thriller or even heist movie, in which the emphasis is on the spectacle of male bodies tested, on the relationship to the Law (even an alternative Law among the thieves), and on the preponderance of a single, privileged point of view. For Jean Larose, the film's distinctiveness is attributable to this refusal of 'cinema' (whereas *Un Zoo la nuit* suffers from an excess of this and a denial of reality) (Larose, 1989). None of the protagonists offers a hero figure to the 'spectator' because they are all 'endowed with too many faults and human qualities to take their cinematographic task to conclusion', and 'defeated because they were not able to defeat themselves, suppress their intimate desires and play their roles of heavies [*durs*]' (Larose, 1989: 27). He thus sees *Pouvoir intime* as 'an allegory of Quebec cinema and the difficulties it has in becoming great [*grand*]' (Larose, 1989: 27) because it symbolizes the tendency in Quebec culture to privilege a debilitating interiority which prevents self-assertion.

On the contrary, I want to argue that *Pouvoir intime* glories in the 'minor' appropriation of cinematic genre. It avoids the Oedipal closures described by Raymond Bellour in relation to Hollywood cinema, which for him

orders and organizes its representations from the position of male heterosexual desire occupied by director, protagonist and implied spectator, and
whose narratives are usually characterized by an Oedipal trajectory in which
the hero comes to accept a positive relationship between his desire and
the Law, that is in marriage (cf. Bergstrom, 1979). *Pouvoir intime* actively
discredits these structures, as father and son self-destruct and a heterosexual couple is decisively not formed and desire not reintegrated into the
Law. The phallic knife and gun are rejected by Roxanne and Janvier, who
are at the end deterritorialized, single people without a centre but nonetheless 'plugged all the more into a social field with multiple connections'
(Deleuze and Guattari, 1986: 70). While the film has relatively few point of
view shots, they are highly multiple, a fact emphasized by the rapid cutting
in the three crisis scenes when a gun is fired. If anything, it is Roxanne who
is privileged, in the low angle shot that introduces her, and in her role as
voyeur as she learns of Martial and Janvier's relationship in the *men's*
toilets.

   Larose's use of 'role' suggests another fundamental way in which the film
renders inoperative any 'major' use of the genre, namely the foreground-
ing of performance. The hideout is a theatre warehouse full of props,
dummies and masks which also recall the early panoramic shot of Roxanne
and Gildor at the station, meeting beneath the cenotaph juxtaposed with
the marginal, drunken down and out. Roxanne has to change her hairstyle
because for Théo she does not look the part, she is not 'feminine' enough.
The crooked guard has the equivalent of stagefright. Roxanne and Janvier
make their escape from the building via the stage, the empty theatre shot
from their point of view. Rather than fixed and naturalized connections
being made between action and masculinity, *Pouvoir intime* proclaims the
provisionality in performance and repetition of all social identities, including memory, if we recall the cenotaph and Martial's contemplation of the
photographs of his couple (at the robbery, there is a cut from one holiday
snap to the hoarding advertising the tropics behind Roxanne). In turn, it
creates a distinct kind of spectatorship. On the one hand it provides the
suspense associated with the genre, in which the viewing subject is caught
in the play of process and position, incoherence and fixity and organized
so by the narrative. On the other hand, it takes away any confirmation or
mastery implied by that trajectory through the surprising and innovative
ending, the reflexive *mise en scène*, and the ambiguous relationship between
a universalizing discourse of human frailty (and by extension, Quebec's
national diffidence) and the heterogeneous positions being represented.

Significantly, *Pouvoir intime* does not attempt to render the surviving identities in major mode. Its representation of homosexuality is distinct, needless to say, from the abjections of *Un Zoo la nuit*, but nor is there any suggestion that 'gay' or 'queer' is being asserted as a new hegemony. The film renders gay identity in minor mode as well, and this is highly relevant to its portrayal of state power and the line of flight at the end. Roxanne and Janvier are not parading completed identities from which they can oppose the system brought metaphorically to collapse in the previous scenes of the film. On the contrary, they embody deterritorialized but also non-limitative and horizontal relations, not molar entities but molecular potentialities, which break with the verticality of power which has demonstrably depended in the film on father-figures and hierarchical succession. *Pouvoir intime* works with genre to produce an economy of desire and identity which is arguably more radical than that permitted by the ambiguities of 'queer', with its tendency to fall back on to binary oppositions and to constitute a group. Rather, such stable cultural images of unity are rejected in favour of a process of becoming something else, a heist movie becoming a psychological and humanistic art movie (the 'all too human' *pouvoir intime*) becoming a nomadic road movie, a traversing of national cinematic frontiers, groups and couples becoming individuals becoming sets of potentialities. This is not to argue that *Pouvoir intime* completely rejects stability, but rather, in the manner of the national-allegorical tension, that stability is always provisional and in process, consisting of forces of homogenization (the cause and effect linear narrative, the forms of recognition of and address to 'Quebec') and heterogenization. Moreover, while it refuses to focus on a gay identity that must be included in the molar structure of the nation, it is no accident that the gay man and androgynous woman occupy the final scene, for it is their economy which offers an alternative to the Oedipalized impasses of much of Quebec cinema.

Chapter 8

Delirium Cinema or Machines of the Invisible?

Patricia Pisters

*Surely a true cinema can contribute to giving us back reasons to believe in the world
and in vanished bodies? The price to be paid, in cinema as elsewhere, was always
a confrontation with madness.*

(*Deleuze, 1989: 201*)

Introduction: clinical and critical

Contemporary audio-visual media culture questions our conception of and
relationship to the image. Cinema, as part of this larger image culture,
seems in need of a theoretical approach that can take into account the
abundance and 'madness' of contemporary image culture and what it does
to our perception, memory and imagination. The increasing amount of
'mind-game'-films and other types of cinema that confuse the difference
between the actual and the virtual, are an important indication of this 'madness'. A schizoanalytic approach, as proposed by Deleuze and Guattari,
might be one way to deal with multiple 'image realities' of our world. In
this essay I examine the ways in which Deleuze and Guattari have related
their philosophy to clinical schizophrenia. Then, I look at two films that
deal with schizophrenic patients in a psychiatric hospital, the Algerian documentary *Alienations* (Malek Bensmail, 2003) and the German film *The
Princess and the Warrior* (Tom Tykwer, 2000). Finally I argue that a schizoanalysis of cinema is necessary to take into account the changes in
contemporary image culture in which cinema is becoming increasingly a
'machine of the invisible' as opposed to the 'machine of the visible' it used
to be. By relating clinical schizophrenia to a critical film theory I'm inspired
by Deleuze's *Essays Critical and Clinical* in which he analyses great works of
art as delirious processes, related to Life and critical creation as well as to
Death and clinical stasis.

Deleuze and Guattari make a very clear distinction between schizophrenia as a pathological disease and schizophrenia as a process (strategy). It is schizophrenia as a process that is the primary focus. In *Anti-Oedipus* schizophrenia is described as 'a potentially revolutionary and liberating flow'; as 'a free form of overcoding and overinvesting libidinal desire'; and also as 'the immanent system of production and anti-production' (schizophrenization), related to 'capitalisms awesome schizophrenic production of energy' (Deleuze and Guattari, 1984: 34). In *A Thousand Plateaus* schizoanalysis is another term for rhizomatics, experimenting in the creation of a Body without Organs and all kind of becomings (Deleuze and Guattari, 1988: 13, 22, 150). So, already from the beginning the question of what is schizoanalysis for Deleuze and Guattari is not answerable with one unique definition.

Nevertheless schizophrenia as a process is derived from schizophrenia as a disease. They are at least related in the sense that both are escape mechanisms from things too unbearable to sustain. The fundamental issue that defines the borderline between 'schizophrenia as a process' and 'schizophrenia as a disease' is, Deleuze and Guattari argue, how to avoid the 'breakthrough' turns into a 'breakdown' (Deleuze and Guattari, 1984: 362). In their own frequent returns to schizophrenia as a disease they demonstrate this border as a very fine line, which is where I start my investigations.

Clinical schizophrenia as a brain disorder

Let me first look at schizophrenia as it is described in neurobiology. It is significant to note from the beginning that schizophrenia is an organic *brain* disease and not an emotional disorder or neurosis (one of the main psychoanalytic diseases). Since Deleuze has argued that 'the brain is the screen' and that film philosophers should look at the biology of the brain, schizophrenia might be one of these areas to look for new 'models' of thinking the image (Deleuze, 2000: 365–73). A clinical diagnosis of schizophrenia is based on behavioural observations and self-reported abnormal mental experiences. Symptoms of schizophrenia are conventionally divided into 'positive' and 'negative' types. Positive symptoms include (paranoid) delusions, hallucinations (often auditory), thought disorder and incoherent verbal expression and bizarre behaviour (all related to a feeling of 'too much' of everything, very energetic, frantic). Negative symptoms include emotional flattening, social withdrawal, apathy, impaired judgement, difficulties in problem solving and poor initiative (all related to a lack of energy, to the point of catatonic collapse). Most forms of schizophrenia show a combination (in various degrees) of several of these symptoms.

Modern neuro-imaging techniques have given us new insights in what happens in a schizophrenic brain but the interpretation of these visualizations of what happens inside the head are disputed. Some neurobiologists argue that virtually every brain region is affected in schizophrenia (Pearlson, 2000: 558). Another hypothesis is that the problem is more significantly to be related to the neurotransmitters and the failure of certain specific areas of the brain to connect very well. The key assumption in this 'disconnection hypothesis' is that the pathophysiology of schizophrenia is expressed in terms of abnormal connections. In a schizophrenic brain the integration and adaptation of sensorimotoric, emotional and cognitive functions are impaired. This is probably due to a failure of integrating signals from the (sensorimotoric) prefrontal regions and the temporal cortices. The synaptic connections are in a continual state of flux, implying time-dependent changes in connectivity that do not function very well in the schizophrenic brain (Friston, 1998: 118). Eugene Bleuler, who introduced the term 'schizophrenia' in 1908 referred to a split in the proper functioning of the brain, a mental splitting (nothing to do with 'split' or 'multiple personality' syndrome but with connections between brain functions). Of course I am not going to interfere in neurobiological debates but interesting connections to a possible schizoanalysis of cinema can be made as I will try to show in what follows.

Two poles of schizophrenia as a process

In *Anti-Oedipus*, and in the posthumously published collection of articles *Two Regimes of Madness*, Deleuze and Guattari distinguish two poles of schizophrenia, two poles in the schizophrenic delirium. One is the machinic pole, or the pole of the machine-organ. Deleuze and Guattari argue that the schizophrenic shows what the unconscious really is, namely a factory full of machinic connections. They recall Bruno Bettelheim's story of little Joey who 'can live, eat, defecate and sleep only if he is plugged into machines provided with motors, wires, lights, carburetors, propellers and steering wheels: an electric feeding-machine, a car-machine that enables him to breathe' (Deleuze and Guattari, 1984:37). 'Connecticut, Connect-I-Cut!' . . . Deleuze and Guattari summarize Joey's machinic desire, and they explain further:

Every machine functions as a break in the flow in relation to the machine to which it is connected, but at the same time it is also a flow itself, or the production of a flow, in relation to the machine connected to it. (. . .) Everywhere there are break-flows out of which desire wells up, thereby constituting its productivity and continually grafting the process of production onto the product. (Deleuze and Guattari, 1984: 36–37)

Deleuze and Guattari give a very positive reading of the disorders of little Joey's autism – more like the Dadaist would make all kind of wild connections – but their point is clear: machinic and unexpected connections are important in schizophrenia. Especially the break-flows with and escape from the psychoanalytic family triangle are emphasized by Deleuze and Guattari. It is not difficult to recognize here the translation of the positive symptoms of clinical schizophrenia into a process to investigate the libidinal economy of the social field.

The other pole is the pole of the Body without Organs. The Body without Organs relates to a rupture of the normal organization of the organs. It organizes the organism differently: 'Why not walk on your head, sing with your sinuses, see through your skin, breathe with your belly', Deleuze and Guattari propose most famously in *A Thousand Plateaus* (Deleuze and Guattari, 1988:151). But the BwO is also the zero degree model of death: 'It is catatonic schizophrenia that gives its model to death. Zero intensity. The death model appears when the body without organs repels the organs and lays them aside: no mouth, no tongue, no teeth – to the point of self-mutilation, to the point of suicide' (Deleuze and Guattari, 1984: 329). This pole can be related to the negative symptoms of clinical schizophrenia, recognized by Deleuze and Guattari as such when they refer to the BwO as catatonic schizophrenia, and hence also to the end of schizophrenia as a process. Here we see how Deleuze and Guattari actually stay very close to clinical schizophrenia but turn it into a new approach towards life and art.

I have to add two other very important aspects that Deleuze and Guattari relate to schizophrenia – and here they move away from the symptoms to the actual experience and the content of the deliriums. First of all, what seems to be very important is that schizophrenia is related to a sensation of intensity or becoming: 'I *feel* that I'm becoming-woman, I *feel* that I'm becoming-God, I *feel* that I'm becoming a clairvoyant, I *feel* that I'm becoming pure matter' (Deleuze, 2003: 21). So consequently the affective dimension should have an important place in schizophrenia as a process as well.

Finally, it is important to emphasize that every delirium is not so much related to the Oedipal theatre, but very much connected to the feeling of a 'too much of history'. The delirium 'concocts' races, civilizations, cultures,

continents, kingdoms, powers, wars, classes and revolutions: all delirium is
socio-political and economic or world-historical, Deleuze and Guattari
argue (Deleuze, 2003: 25). Again Deleuze and Guattari stay close to the
experiences of real schizophrenics but they turn it into something positive – mostly defined as a way out of the psychoanalytic familial matrix.

Alienations: schizophrenia as universal symptom of 'Madness'

Moving from definitions of schizoanalysis to cinema, I now first want to
investigate how schizoanalysis as a disease can be related to films that deal
specifically with this brain disorder. In the last section I draw on the wider
implications for cinema and film theory, and hence for the schizoanalytic
status of contemporary audio-visual culture more generally.

Malek Bensmail's documentary *Alienations* (2003) in which the filmmaker
follows doctors and patients of a mental hospital in Constantine (Algeria)
in many ways seems to confirm everything Deleuze and Guattari say a
bout schizophrenia. We find both poles of schizophrenia: the connecting
'machine-bodies' of the patients who, especially in their speech, connect
everything in a seemingly wild way, and their catatonic BwOs to the point of
suicidal death wishes. The film opens with a beautiful scene of a girl who
is having a conversation in French with (what later on appears to be) a
doctor. Explaining that she has degrees in biology, medicine, law, veterinary
medicine and that she speaks seven languages, she concludes she *feels*
she has supernatural and metaphysical powers. She also *feels* she is helped
by six Muslims to protect her from the attacks she has to suffer from people
at the faculty. So the intensity of the feeling and the abundance of energy
that Deleuze and Guattari speak of (related to the positive symptoms of
schizophrenia) are clearly present.

In another scene male patients have a group conversation. One of the
patients starts a discourse about America, which he ends by singing 'We are
the World'. He speaks a mixture of French and Arabic. The confusion of his
languages gets lost in translation but in terms of contents he states:

'Now, you have to remember this: you were told "we are the world – we
are the children". Don't cut me off when I'm speaking.'

'Yes! But I want to say something else. Why is America bombing Iraq,
bombing Iraq, bombing Iraq. Iraq has never asked anything of them.
They want everything from the whole world because they sing "we are the

world we are the children". We are all brothers. Even the pacific Jews, I'm with them.'

In this scene, several things are noticeable. First of all, the confusion of languages is striking. No language is spoken very well. This is a well-known symptom of schizophrenia, but it is also very much a general (schizo-phrenic) problem in Algeria, which since independence has only partially and quite unsystematically replaced the previously French educational system with Arabic. Second, the world-historical dimensions of the discourse are striking. World politics, war in Iraq, Jews and many more elements are all connected (Connect-I-Cut) in one discourse. But like the language aspect, it is actually not so very strange because world politics is also what overwhelms the 'sane' people, causing feelings of despair and anxiety. We can all recognize these feelings in some form or another. Third, the impression of mutual respect between doctors and patients is significant. There appears to be a bond between doctors and patients only separated by a small degree of sanity (or perhaps a white coat). Apart from the world politics mentioned here, it is very clear that many patients have deep wounds from the civil war in Algeria during the 1990s, when nobody's life was secure. Victims and perpetrators are equally afflicted and together in this clinic. Fourth, the role of the camera itself cannot be ignored. The camera is not a 'fly on the wall' but is clearly addressed. Sometimes the patients speak to the director directly and they are very conscious of what is being filmed. The filmmaker is implicated in the process of filming, what Deleuze has called the 'mutual-becoming' of filmmaker and characters in the modern political film.

What we actually see here is that doctors, patients and filmmakers are all implicated in the same world, which is very touching and implies the spectator as well. It is also our world. Going back to Deleuze and Guattari we can conclude that they are right to argue that the delirium is moving between machinic and catatonic poles, that it is world-historical and socio-political, and that many elements of the schizo are actually also part of our daily experiences – especially the *feeling* of being overwhelmed by world politics (which is enhanced by the increasing amount of audio-visual data).

Intercultural perspective on schizophrenia

There is something else at stake and here as well. When we look at the film from a perspective of cultural specificity (cultural differences), the socius, the political, is always the prime target and source of the deliriums of the patients in this Algerian clinic. However, Algeria, like all Arabic countries has a collective culture where there is no room for individual problems or traumas in the first place, and this, according to Malek Bensmail, is actually the most fundamental problem for these patients: they always blame the government (Bouteflika and older presidents are frequently mentioned). Nobody starts looking at the level of the individual, or near home. In collective cultures like Algeria, thinking on an individual level could be an important line of flight (which does not automatically mean forgetting about the world-political).

In this respect, something remarkable happened in the film. The patient just quoted, later on in the film confesses to Bensmail's camera a personal childhood trauma of sexual abuse, something he never told the doctors. This is remarkable because these things are never told in collective cultures because it's a huge taboo – and one could argue that the camera in this case helps to individualize this patient.[1] So here we run into a possible limitation of the Deleuzian model of schizophrenia if we try to universalize it. For Deleuze and Guattari the enemy is psychoanalysis' insistence on the individual, Oedipus and the family. Everything they positively argue for in *Anti-Oedipus* in respect to schizoanalysis, is negatively connoted in respect to psychoanalysis. For instance, they argue that the first reason for a 'breakthrough' to turn into a clinical 'breakdown' is neurotization and oedipalization: 'First the process is arrested, the limit of desiring-production is displaced, travestied, and now passes into the Oedipal subaggregate. So the schizo is effectively neurotised, and it is this neurotisation that constitutes his illness' (Deleuze and Guattari, 1984: 363).

Now looking at western films about schizophrenia, it is apparent that Deleuze and Guattari are absolutely right. The film *Princess and the Warrior* (Tom Tykwer, 2000) for instance, clearly shows how the main character, Sissi, breaks free from her literally mad family. Sissi is born in a psychiatric hospital and has lived there all her life. She is one of the doctors, but she too is very close to the patients. When she falls in love with Bodo (in an amazingly strong scene in which he saves her life following a car accident by piercing her throat with a straw enabling her to breathe) it is the beginning of her breakthrough out of the 'mad family'. They literally take a 'line of flight' that sets them free when at the end of the film they jump together from the roof of the clinic and escape. This scene is very 'anti-oedipal' indeed since one of the patients (in love with Sissi) as a very jealous Oedipal son tried to kill 'the father' (Bodo, as lover of Sissi) by throwing an electric bread toaster into Bodo's bath tub. So here, it certainly could be argued that breaking open the family is liberating. At various points in the film the patients are invited to go out for a walk, which is virtually quoting *Anti-Oedipus'* slogan that 'a schizophrenic out for a walk is a better model than a neurotic lying on the analyst's couch' (Deleuze and Guattari, 1984: 2).

Looking at *Alienations* however, we have to conclude that things are more complicated than that and that perhaps Deleuze and Guattari are creating too simple a binary opposition between psychoanalysis and schizoanalysis, between the family and the socius. Here the patient's personal confession about a childhood trauma might just as well be a breakthrough (and not automatically a neurotization), and seeing and feeling in *Alienations* the longing for a family, for a mother and a father, is so overwhelmingly part of the patient's desires that it cannot be overlooked. I should emphasize that I am saying this not to argue that we should go back to Oedipal psycho-analysis *pur sang* – the shortcomings of the Oedipal model as a matrix are obvious and well demonstrated by Deleuze and Guattari (and others). I also do not want to deny the imprisoning family structures that are also part of a collective society (cf. revenge of honour/blood revenge). But the principle of the family as part in the whole network of connections and desires should not be overlooked. Deleuze and Guattari do acknowledge the existence of Oedipal relations and have argued that they just want to break open the Oedipal theatre to add other dimensions. But the fact is that there is a strong oppositional tendency towards anything related to the nuclear family – which in the western context of the second half of the twentieth century was very understandable. But in a contemporary intercultural, transnational context things are even more complicated. It is clear that the notion of the family itself has changed through emancipation and migration.[2] In collective cultures the individual and the family have a different sense altogether. So, when proposing schizoanalysis as a contem-porary model (for thinking and for cinema) we should not 'throw out the baby with the bathwater' by adhering rigidly to the binary opposition between psychoanalysis and schizoanalysis.

Schizoanalytic film theory

So what could all this possibly mean for film analysis and film theory? Again I will stay close to schizophrenia as a disease and look for the rare moments where Deleuze does mention schizophrenia in the cinema books. I will take these moments as cues for more general principles of a schizoanalysis of cinema. To my knowledge there are only two instances in the cinema books where Deleuze refers explicitly to schizophrenia. The first is in

The Movement-Image – particularly and significantly in the chapters on the affection-image. This is right after Deleuze has distinguished two figures or types of affection-images (two types of firstness): the power-quality expressed by a face or an equivalent; and the power-quality represented in any-space-whatever. Deleuze then discusses the particular 'system of emotions' that the affection-image makes us enter into. He then says:

> The young schizophrenic experiences his 'first feelings of unreality' before two images: that of a comrade who draws near and whose face enlarges exaggeratedly (one might say like a lion); that of a field of corn which becomes boundless dazzling yellow immensity. (Deleuze, 1985: 110)

This is only a small remark but one that seems to be very relevant in respect to the question of a schizoanalysis of cinema. The importance of affect and feeling in clinical schizophrenia is already mentioned: the young woman in *Alienations* feels she is being protected by six Muslims. More importantly both *Alienations* and *The Princess and the Warrior* are full of affection-images: face/close-up & any-space-whatever / hand (tactile images of Bresson). From a schizoanalytic perspective, it might be argued that affect seems to be a fundamental element of cinema, not just related to the movement-image but as a general feeling of all types of images (especially in contemporary cinema).

Here we can make a difference with psychoanalytic film theory. In psychoanalytic film theory emotions are channelled through identification with the protagonist's desires and motivations. In schizoanalytic film theory the affect touches us *as affect,* very often without any identification. We are dealing much more with a feeling that touches us perhaps because we recognize it on a world-historical level, including personal experiences and memories. Schizoanalysis of cinema always takes account of the *power of the affect.*

The second mentioning of schizophrenia is at the end of the *Time-Image.* When Deleuze discusses sound as a component of the image, the conversational nature of schizophrenia and the schizophrenic nature of conversation is mentioned in respect to the Hollywood talkie (sound cinema) that Deleuze defines as 'an art of sociability and encounter with the other that passes through conversation':

> [Conversation] possesses the power of artificially subordinating all these determinations (. . .). Interests, feelings or love no longer determine conversation; they themselves depend on the division of stimulation in

conversation, the latter determining relations of force and structurations which are particular to it. This is why there is always something mad, schizophrenic in a conversation taken for itself (with bar conversations, lovers conversations, money conversations, or small talk as its essence). (Deleuze, 1989: 230)

We have seen in clinical diagnoses of schizophrenia how constant chatter is one of the positive symptoms of schizophrenia. *Alienations* shows as well the fundamental place of conversation in schizophrenia. But coming to think of conversation and the way it can take its own course, it can indeed alienate us quite easily (and thus has something mad even in normal situations). Again Deleuze's remark in the *Time-Image* is made in passing, but I think again this remark relates to something fundamental in respect to a schizoanalysis of cinema. It addresses the way in which Deleuze conceives of cinema as a very powerful speech act, in the sense that it has actual power to do something (or to 'operate in reality'). This *power of the speech* act I would determine as another important element of schizoanalytic film theory.

Then a final essential characteristics of schizoanalysis of cinema, is related to the time-image in general. Several aspects of the time-image relate to 'symptoms' of schizophrenia. One of the characteristics of the time-image is that it makes us grasp 'something too intolerable and unbearable, too powerful, too unjust, sometimes too beautiful' (Deleuze, 1989: 18). This is like the 'too much of everything' that the schizophrenic feels and which is a fundamental characteristic of our contemporary saturated world where there is always too much (or too little) of everything: 'A purely optical and sound situation does not extend into action, any more than it is induced by an action. It makes us grasp, it is supposed to make us grasp, something intolerable and unbearable. (. . .) It is a matter of something too powerful, or too unjust, but sometimes also too beautiful, and which henceforth outstrips our sensory-motor capacities' (Deleuze, 1989: 18).

Another schizophrenic aspect of the time-image is its seemingly disconnected character: the weak sensory-motor connections enable 'wild' connections to be made. As Deleuze argues in respect to Ozu (referring to Leibniz): 'It is just that we have to admit that, because the linkages of the terms in the series are naturally weak, they are constantly upset and do not appear in order. An ordinary term goes out of sequence, and emerges in the middle of another sequence of ordinary things in relation to which it takes on the appearance of a strong moment, a remarkable or complex point' (Deleuze, 1989: 5). In this way, the time-image actually connects to the schizophrenic brain which 'disconnects' or makes false connections, out of normal connections (as mentioned earlier in the 'disconnection hypothesis' in neurobiology).

The new psychological automaton that Deleuze distinguishes in the time-image also corresponds to the schizo: characters that are no longer driven by psychologically motivated motor action, but are defined in relation to the affects they can trigger (even by completely artificial means, cf. Club Silencio scene in *Mulholland Drive*), speech acts they provide (Bresson's models) and feedback loops they enter into (Resnais's zombies, as Deleuze calls them). In Resnais, Deleuze argues, there are no more flashbacks but rather feedbacks and failed feedbacks (Deleuze, 1989: 266). They all seem to be disconnected (alienated) of themselves. With the catatonic BwO of the schizo as degree zero, they become like 'transmitters' of affects and speech acts.

In the time-image Deleuze has demonstrated extensively how the virtual and the actual start chasing each other to the point where they become indistinguishable. The most interesting aspect of this indiscernibility or undecidability between virtual and actual (dream and reality, past and present, true and false) is that it endows the virtual with reality. Deleuze has argued that movement-images give us material aspects of subjectivity, while time-images give us immaterial aspects of subjectivity. Time-images show us the *power of the virtual,* which is a mental reality, but a reality nevertheless, and again, this is a fundamentally characteristic of the schizophrenic delirium: even though it is not actual, it is very real.

The brain is the screen: cinema as 'Machine of the Invisible'

To conclude these thoughts about possible elements of a schizoanalysis of cinema, I would like to suggest that Deleuze's idea that 'the brain is the screen' can be developed into a schizoanalysis of cinema that can take account of the madness of contemporary audio-visual culture. Schizophrenia as a clinical disease and the schizophrenic brain provide useful clues for understanding the implication of schizoanalysis of cinema, which seems to become increasingly important in contemporary cinema that is characterized by chaos, 'wild' connections, immersive overload of the senses, ambiguity, confusion and affect. The delirium of the schizo is world-historical in the first place, but as a critical note I have suggested that we should avoid reinstating a binary opposition between the world-historical schizo and the individual trauma of the family in psychoanalysis. Especially when we move Deleuze across cultures – as I have tried to demonstrate by comparing *Alienations* to *Princess and the Warrior* – this becomes an important pitfall to avoid. Having said this, it is clear that schizoanalytic film theory has a very different focus to psychoanalytic film theory. As I suggested it has as its three main elements *the power of affect, the power of the speech act and the power of the virtual.* Importantly, these are all elements of Deleuze's cinema books, but schizoanalytic as well. But distinguishing the power of affect, the speech act and the virtual are basic elements of schizoanalysis, and it should be clear that these elements cut across movement-images and time-images alike, albeit at different speeds and intensities.[3] Hence this implies that the opposition between movement-image and time-image no longer holds in absolute terms (only in gradual terms), especially when we look at contemporary cinema.

To conclude I would like to argue that the 'schizoanalytic turn' is related to a paradigm shift in film theory in which cinema as a 'machine of the visible' has become a 'machine of the invisible'. The Apparatus Theory, related to the psychoanalytic turn developed in the seventies and eighties, considered cinema as a 'machine of the visible'. As Jean-Louis Commoli argued cinema as a 'machines of the visible' produces an 'impression of reality':

> Directly and totally programmed by the ideology of resemblance, of the 'objective' duplication of the 'real' itself conceived as a specular reflection, cinema technology occupied itself in improving and refining the initial imperfect dispositif, always imperfect by the ideological delusion produced by the film as 'impression of reality'. (Commoli, 1980: 133)

In other words, cinema in the 'old paradigm' is conceived as a machine that takes literally 'impressions of reality' and gives us re-presentations of reality. Cinema belongs to the 'regime of the visible' which enhances our perception of the material world.[4] The difference with Deleuze's conception of cinema, especially in its time-image characteristics is noticeable: 'This is the very special extension of the opsign: to make time and thought perceptible, to make them visible and of sound' (Deleuze, 1989: 18). By entering into our brain/mind, cinema has become, what I would like to call, a *machine of the invisible*. This paradigm shift also demands that we no longer consider cinema an 'illusion of reality' but rather a 'reality of illusion'. It involves a shift from considering cinema and the spectator as a 'disembodied eye' (defined by the look and the gaze, desire and identification) to considering cinema and the spectator as an embodied brain (defined by perceptions – even illusory ones –, selections – even random ones –, memories – even fake ones – , imaginations, suggestions and above all emotions as pure affect). The embodied nature of the brain and the physical aspect or quality of the brain is very important to notice as well. In any case this is related to a final characteristic of the paradigm shift which is the shift from considering the spectator in front of a spectacle (screen), to a spectator embedded – immersed in an audio-visual environment in which filmmaker/camera, characters and spectators, world and screens are all chasing and questioning each other and where we have to ask ourselves constantly: where is the screen?

In this sense I think it is also interesting to note that, speaking in Foucauldian terms, schizoanalysis also marks a new episteme. In the nineteenth century and first half of the twentieth century madness was defined in psychoanalytic terms and was considered to be a disease that separated the sane from the insane. However, if one suffered from an individual traumatic experience in childhood this was, in final analysis, most of the times curable – at least that was the general assumption. In the schizoanalytic episteme sanity and insanity are much closer and less easily distinguishable because of the shared 'feeling' of living in a 'mad world'. It is also less easily curable . . . The difference between the dream in *Spellbound* (Hitchcock, 1945), which is clearly distinguished from reality, interpretable and curable, and the delirious mis-en-scene of *Mulholland Drive* (Lynch, 2001) in which dream and reality, sanity and insanity are more difficult to distinguish and understand and remain mostly ambiguously enfolded in each other, is an exemplary case in point. The epistemological uncertainties that the schizoanalytic episteme entails, puts choice and belief (the choice to believe) before knowledge. As Deleuze has put it: 'The question is no longer: does cinema give us the illusion of the world? But: how does cinema restore our belief in the world?' (Deleuze 1989: 181–2).[5]

Of course, the important question remains: how to avoid a breakthrough turning into a breakdown? As I have suggested this is not just achieved by avoiding the family or by immediately going into the world-historical. Since schizoanalysis is so closely related to the mysteries of the brain, and since the brain and the screen are now so fundamentally entangled, we should perhaps look more deeply into neurobiology as Deleuze suggested in 'The Brain is the Screen'. But of course we will never understand all of the brain's mysteries. So more pragmatically, all we can do to contain the power of thoughts (the power of the invisible) to manageable proportions is perhaps to learn how to 'put our mind on a diet' as John Nash in *A Beautiful Mind* (Ron Howard, 2001) chooses to do in order to live with his schizophrenic brain. Or, as Deleuze would put it: to develop strategies to turn madness into metaphysics.

Chapter 9

Off Your Face: Schizoanalysis, Faciality and Film

Anna Powell

For Deleuze and Guattari, 'dismantling the face' is 'a politics, involving real becoming, an entire becoming-clandestine' (Deleuze and Guattari, 1988: 188). This chapter explores the operations of the cinematic face and suggest its schizoanalytical potential. Aesthetics are viral in nature, being known 'not through representation, but through *affective* contamination' (Guattari, 1995: 92). I argue that, via facial mutation, schizo cinema breaks down our immune defences, infecting and living in us on all levels, sprouting new growths of sensation, perception and thought.

Deleuze consistently asserts that 'the brain is the screen' and that cinema is a powerful mode of thought (Deleuze, 2000: 366). In the film event, screen and viewer become one. Rather than revisiting the art-house faciality of Deleuze's solo Cinema Books here, I suggest ways in which Deleuze and Guattari's schizoanalysis can be set to rethink faciality and I exemplify this in a brief analysis of a recent science-fiction/drugs film, *A Scanner Darkly* (Richard Linklater, 2006).

So why choose a mainstream movie for schizoanalysis? Art-house films self-consciously set out to emphasize cinematography as a technique for elucidating psychological or philosophical trajectories. Some of the work of rethinking cinema has, arguably, already been done for us by directors who offer ready-made methods of self-reflexivity for adoption. They pass pre-digested cinematic thoughts over to us via non-linear time, multiple narratives, subjective camerawork and expressive colour. We are invited to share second- and third-order insights already worked through beforehand.

Mainstream fantasy films, as popular box-office entertainment, reach a wider audience than the art-house. Some popular films can, I argue, challenge us because formulaic characters, conventional narrative patterns and simple moral messages actually demand more creative input. Overloaded visuals or lack of narrative complexity invite us to fill out flatness or pare down redundancy by thinking in new ways.

Science-fiction film frequently draws on literary originals already packed with challenging ideas, such as the novels of Philip K. Dick. But the constraints of budget, box-office and running time demand broad brushstrokes and thematic simplification. Hollywood formulas privilege action narratives and spectacular effects. Yet, I argue, it is in these same reductions, exaggerations and simplifications that we can discover twisted literalizations of Deleuze and Guattari's ideas and engage with the questions they open up.

Schizoanalysis asserts the machinic connection of the embodied brain and the textual body. Deleuze and Guattari distinguish the 'machinic' from mechanism's closed sets. Like the human body itself, film techniques participate in dynamic forces mobilized by the machinery of projection and viewing. Sci-fi produces new machines that can become machinic assemblages. Melding biology and technology in robotics and prosthesis, sci-fi entities are not limited by conventional body maps. The genre not only focuses on cyborgs, androids and artificial intelligences, but also presents the genetically engineered brain as a transmutation machine and speculates on the kind of thought that might drive such a brain.

Sci-fi film, then, is both overtly mechanical and potentially machinic. Here, faces play an important part. My main interest in mutating facial images lies in their use-value as affective stimuli for more adventurous ways of thinking through cinema. On the domestic DVD or computer as well as on the big screen, we discover fugitive faces that elude subjective or social fixation.

My chosen example also foregrounds drugs. Like sci-fi, films 'about' drugs (particularly hallucinogens) offer an ideal opportunity for the expressive powers of special effects to alter consensual reality. They also shift focus from linear plot development and character interaction to spectacle. Drugs films use extreme facial transmutation to make mental effects manifest and enable the viewer to share intoxication. In David Cronenberg's *The Naked Lunch* (1991) and Terry Gilliam's *Fear and Loathing in Las Vegas* (1998) characters hallucinate monsters in grotesque close-up.

There is a strand of sci-fi that uses drugs imagery in tandem with other modes of alterity wrought by science. Although no drugs are visibly ingested, the kaleidescopic Stargate sequence in Stanley Kubrick's *2001: A Space Odyssey* (1968) is widely acknowledged as 'cinematic LSD' in its affect on the viewer in bending space and time. Ken Russell's *Altered States* (1981) showcases drastic facial alteration as Jessup, the renegade scientist, uses himself as experimental subject. His mutations from Neanderthal proto-human to metallic *übermensch* results from the genetic regression induced by hallucinogenic fungi. Here, I use schizoanalysis to highlight and intensify facial 'dismantling' via the dual impact of a more recent drug-fuelled sci-fi film.

Schizoanalysis, psychoanalysis, film analysis

So what can schizoanalysis offer us as a way of responding to the event of film? How does it differ from psychoanalytic methods applied to cinema from the mid-1970s on? Although they still acknowledge the role of fantasy in shaping perception of the external world, Deleuze and Guattari attack the paternalistic structures of Freudianism. Seeking to dismantle, reverse and renew it, schizoanalysis operates as '*the outside of psychoanalysis itself* which can only be revealed through an internal reversal of its analytical categories' (Deleuze and Guattari, 1984: 139).

Oedipus contributes to the existing sociolinguistic system. In *Anti-Oedipus*, Deleuze and Guattari draw on Nietzsche and Bergson to develop schizoanalysis as a new concept of mental and emotional immanence not centred on personal subjectivity. Psychoanalytic film theory approaches the film text – or the generalized spectator – from an 'archaeological' perspective. This unearths symbolic scenarios on screen (and in implied viewers) as psychosexual traces of the mother/father/child Oedipal triangle. As the 'talking cure' cinepsychoanalysis is language based and draws on structural linguistics to read moving images as though they were text. Instead of digging up symbols of the past, schizoanalysis is a dynamic approach to life in process. It helps us explore the affect of film *as* experience.

In breaking free from Freud's paranoid Oedipal structures, schizoanalysis develops a new map of body and psyche, the Body without Organs (BwO). Fluid and shifting, this body in process draws on the pre-subjective mental and emotional forces of the 'orphan unconscious' (Deleuze and Guattari, 1984: 81). Privileging ongoing experience as 'intensive voyage' it leaves familiar physical and mental spaces behind in a radical cartography of deterritorialization (Deleuze and Guattari, 1984: 319). BwOs do not need parents to define their identity for them. Neither are they limited to the gendered, genital sexuality that Freudian film theory discovers in all movies, but are autoproductive desiring machines with 'a thousand tiny sexes'.

Schizoanalysis is broadly applicable to rethinking politics as well as art. It seeks to reach regions of the psyche '"beyond all law" – where the problem of Oedipus can no longer be raised' (Deleuze and Guattari, 1984: 81–2).

The 'schizo' is not limited to a narcissistic state of entropy, but is firmly located in the collective machinery of the social as a disruptive force that can spread. Both Freudian and Lacanian psychoanalysis claim that lack and split subjectivity are inevitable human conditions. They disempower us by teaching ways to adjust to primal loss. Deleuze and Guattari counter this by exploding the hierarchical structures of psychic interiority by the immanent force of schizoanalytical desire. Ideas become dynamic events or lines of flight, thought by a self always in process (Kennedy, 2000: 69). Schizoanalysis offers us a fluid, inclusive and optimistic micropolitics of desire.

Schizoanalysis, schizophrenia, art and madness

At first glance, Deleuze and Guattari appear to be encouraging us to adopt or at least imitate a kind of madness. They do not interpret mental anomalies as the psychopathology of early trauma. Instead, they focus on dynamic new transitions experienced in intensive states. At this point, it is important to distinguish schizoanalysis and schizophrenia. Jean Laplanche and J. B. Pontalis classically define schizophrenia in terms of clinical pathology. For them, this incoherent state involves 'discordance, dissociation, disintegration', accompanied by detachment from reality, 'a turning in upon the self and the predominance of a delusional mental life given over to the production of phantasies (autism) and ultimately intellectual and affective "deterioration"' (Laplanche and Pontalis, 1988: 408).

This actual, clinical condition is acknowledged, but also reconsidered by Deleuze and Guattari. Their aesthetico/political critique distinguishes clinical schizophrenia from schizoanalysis and its 'schizo'. For them, schizos are experimental artists such as Samuel Beckett, Antonin Artaud, Arthur Rimbaud and Franz Kafka. The schizo is idealized as 'a free man, irresponsible, solitary, and joyous, finally able to say and do something simple in his own name, without asking permission, a desire lacking nothing, a flux that overcomes barriers and codes, a name that no longer designates any ego whatever' (Deleuze and Guattari, 1984: 131). Despite the apparently existentialist emphasis on free will, their model unravels romantic individualism. It also diverges sharply from the psychoanalytic view that fantasy enables the return of the repressed, ultimately engineering sublimation and social consensus.

For Deleuze and Guattari, pleasure is materially based in immanent sensation. Desire, which exceeds the sexual, is not the product of lack, but is a productive and automatic machine. Its autoerotic force extends, infusing the social with desire, in 'the nuptial celebration of a new alliance, a new birth, a radiant ecstasy, as though the eroticism of the machine liberated other unlimited forces' (Deleuze and Guattari, 1984: 18). Such automatism is experienced via intensive states: 'haecceities' (things in themselves) and not 'subjectivities', which produce an 'intense feeling of *transition*' without the static final positions and identities of psychoanalysis (Deleuze and Guattari, 1984: 18).

One schizo plane of transition is pre-verbal affect prior to the structural formation of subjectivity. This offers 'intensive qualities in their pure state, to the point that is almost unbearable [. . .], states of pure, naked intensity stripped of all shape and form' (Deleuze and Guattari, 1984: 18). Here, the 'beyond' of the pleasure principle is not the entropy of the death drive supposed by Freud, but the dynamic flux of sensation itself.

Guattari's input into schizoanalysis drew on his work at La Borde experimental clinic and his radical advocacy of the anti-psychiatry movement. Art therapy was integral to his clinical practice with schizophrenics. In some ways, schizoanalysis is his methodology adapted as a direct approach to the intense encounter with art. *Anti-Oedipus* insists on the political urgency of Guattari's innovations, arguing that 'a materialist psychiatry recognises the state of desire and its production as primary and determinant, whereas an idealist psychiatry rests on ideas and their expression', and emphasizing the machinic practices of desiring-production (Deleuze and Guattari, 1984: 322).

For the schizophrenic, experimental group work gravitates against classic analysis in favour of the dynamic, interactive 'desiring machine, independently of any interpretation' (Deleuze and Guattari, 1984: 322). This discourages any reconstruction of the 'normal' individualistic ego and facilitates a communal group ego. It is fundamentally opposed to Freud's strengthening of the ego to contest the incursions of the id from 'below' and the superego from 'above'.

Deleuze's philosophical contribution to schizoanalysis drew on Bergson's work on the fluid nature of consciousness. In *Time and Free Will*, Bergson outlines a dual topography of the psyche. The outer, extensive crust is spatial and socially oriented, whereas the inner core vibrates intensively in the flux of duration. There are two 'selves', one the external projection and social representation of the other. Internal operations are reached by deep introspection, which 'leads us to grasp our inner states as living things, constantly *becoming*, as states not amenable to measure, which permeate one another' (Bergson, 1971: 231). This model is radically distinct from Freud's tripartite psyche (ego, superego, id). It removes the transference, by which the analyst adopts the parental role during the replay of childhood trauma.

Although both models acknowledge inner complexity, their views of time and psychic interiority differ. For Freud, the unconscious is a timeless zone where the past directly shapes the present in its own image. He asserts time as a purely conscious experience. Unconscious processes are '*timeless* i.e. they are not altered by the passage of time; they have no reference to time at all' (Freud, 1991: 91). Bergson's inner state, though also formed of memory, belongs to the durational process of perpetual becoming. This dynamic and multi-faceted model stresses the change and multiplicity that would become seminal to schizoanalysis. Traditional models of the body's organic layout cannot account for its living force and intensity. Schizoanalysis offers intensive maps of the body's flux, becoming by its own volition. Sensory and cognitive hallucinations arise from this pre-subjective and machinic process, crucial to the production and reception of the arts outside the clinical context.

Schizoanalysis *A Scanner Darkly*

The critical process of schizoanalysis and the figure of the schizo take us on a new route into *A Scanner Darkly*. Although the protagonist could actually be clinically schizophrenic, this is not necessary for schizoanalysis to operate. If film is viewed as a processual experience, characters, style and viewer engage together in a schizo assemblage with an ego-less freedom from constraint.

Deleuze and Guattari insist upon the immanence of art as 'a being in sensation and nothing else: it exists in itself' (Deleuze and Guattari, 1991: 161). Psychic interiority is replaced by the energy of immanent desire. Ideas become dynamic events or 'lines of flight' into 'a fibrous web of directions, much like a map or a tuber' (Kennedy, 2000: 69). The term 'rhizome' (lateral, multi-forked root system) suggests the nomadic movement of thought by a self in process. Schizoanalytic film theory, then, approaches the moving image *in itself*, as experienced event. It does not rely on structures of signification that fix the film's 'meaning'. For schizoanalysis, material capture in space and time replaces representation.

Since Mulvey's 'Visual Pleasure and Narrative Cinema' (1975) psychoanalytic film theory has analysed the sexual politics of the 'gaze'. In doing this, it disregards the creative act of looking as well as other senses engaged in film perception. The look is an embodied sensation, a component in the sensory assemblage that includes 'senses' such as the haptic touch stimulated by film images. We are all human living images engaged in the wider flux of images. Body and mind are a perceptual continuum: we perceive and think what we feel. This machinic assemblage operates for everyone in the audience. All cinema, not just avant-garde texts which foreground their own construction, can be read materially via the sensational event of film viewing. The directness of film springs from its stimulation of the optic nerves, initially agitating the senses before the cognitive and reflective faculties. The camera's technological automatism penetrates and melds with the flux of the material world. It removes perceptual experience from the idealizing tendency of humanist frames of reference. Although the camera is set up, angled and moved by human agency, its ultimately technological apparatus passively records objects before it. This enables it to capture the raw phenomena of matter.

For schizoanalytical film theory, perception is freed from the norms of human cognition. In the case of sci-fi, not bound by the 'slice of life' of classic realism, the virtual sensations induced are often of an unfamiliar kind able to push through subjective boundaries. Psychoanalytic film theory pathologizes disturbing images and aims to strengthen ego defences. From a Deleuze–Guattarian perspective, however, 'madness' may be read in a more positive light. Anomalous states expressed by film can be celebrated, both for their stylistic innovations and their contagious affect on the audience.

Schizo cinema does not fix a set of equations for representation or meanings for symbols. Its aim, according to Deleuze and Guattari's polemics, is to 'overturn the theatre of representation into the order of desiring-production' (Deleuze and Guattari, 1984: 271). The dynamic forces of desire can free us from the habitual templates of representation as we think in new, uncharted ways. Our job as schizo critics is to map assemblages at work in their mutual operations, to meld form, style and content and to identify a film's predominant 'diagrammatic components' each with singular quality and special affective force. So what can we discover via the mutant face and its body?

The Body without Organs, cinematic affect and faciality

The body of schizoanalysis is politically engaged, the 'intensive, anarchist' BwO (Deleuze, 1998: 131). It is by working with this affective body that cinema opens us up to becoming. Impacting on the BwO, cinematic affect undermines spatial and temporal orientation and unravels symbolic hierarchies. The cinematic experience is both visceral and mental. On-screen images are, in one sense, non-material simulacra projected onto a flat screen, yet the viewer-screen assemblage encounters them corporeally and conceptually. They stimulate neuronal networks to biologically quantifiable arousal. But affects and percepts are not limited to organic bodies. Slumped in our cinema seat, or in front of the domestic screen, our customary mind/ body maps become fluid and perceptive BwOs.

The moving images of cinema are not limited by action-based plot. When they exceed the purely functional, the spectator's attention increases and struggles to process the flow of anomalous images. If radically challenged, perceptions give up attempts to fix signification. They themselves become intensive affects in the film assemblage to produce a 'being of the sensory, a being of sensation, on an anorganic plane of composition that is able to restore the infinite' (Deleuze and Guattari, 1991: 302). Impacting both on body and brain, the cinematic event vibrates intensively in us as thought. Deleuze and Guattari figure consciousness as a shifting field of forces with depth as well as surface. In perpetual motion, it moves by 'speed and slowness, floating affects' and 'allows us to "perceive the imperceptible"' (Deleuze and Guattari, 1988: 267). The BwO is a responsive reverberation on the universal plane of images in process. Here, in this non-spatial locale, schizo intensity is moved by non-subjective powers of affect to produce immanent desire. Change and multiplicity are fundamental to schizoanalysis as it works to free us from the representational templates of habit. It seeks anti-authoritarian ends, to overthrow despotic systems that block becoming on all levels. As a BwO the face, animated by 'intensive movements' can be a crucial tool in this process (Deleuze and Guattari, 1988: 171).

Guattari and Deleuze seek to escape the despotic face of the signifier and its fixed meanings. So how does the face signify hierarchies of power and territorial possession? The facial machine produces a continual flow of faces to be read 'according to the changeable combinations of its cogwheels' (Deleuze and Guattari, 1988: 168). Sketches of 'signifying' and 'despotic' faces in *A Thousand Plateaus* such as the 'four-eye machine' of mother/baby dyad, are abstract machines that multiply eyes as despotic surveillance seeks omniscience (Deleuze and Guattari, 1988: 183). The face revolves around the 'white wall/black hole' symbiosis. Its pre-subjective potential is a blank sheet, 'a suggestive whiteness, a hole that captures' (Deleuze and Guattari, 1988: 168). Like a cine film on its screen, significance and subjectification are projected onto this 'white wall', which, as 'the centre of significance to which all of the deterritorialised signs affix themselves', marks their limit (Deleuze and Guattari, 1988: 168). Although the face is potentially without territorial boundaries, the signifier is reterritorialized by the eyes of surveillance and the despotic power of the signifier. Projected onto the face, repressive social and psychoanalytical signification reflects back the 'dreary world of the signifier' with its 'archaism', 'essential deception' and 'profound antics' (Deleuze and Guattari, 1988: 116–17).

The black hole of physics is an imploded star with matter too infinitely dense for even light to escape. As well as emanating an ever-watchful gaze, human black holes also contain repressed consciousness and passion, which, like signifiers, produce their own redundancies (Deleuze and Guattari, 1988: 167). The dense facial machine, then, contains traps. In order to fix signification on the outer world, we must evade being sucked in by our own black holes. An extended kind of white wall/black hole faciality is traditionally engaged in the production and reception processes of art, which territorialize a blank surface, by words on a page, marks on canvas or images on screen, to be deciphered as authoritative text.

Platonism is undermined by schizo faciality. In Plato's World of Forms, the Ideal Form of materially imperfect things is an innate reference point for manifest matter. The fixed, representational view of the face is Platonic, while its overturning reveals a shifting map of affect. The sensational flux of facial response is not representative, but is material affect *in itself.* The face of a fleeing coward in close-up, for instance, functions as cowardice itself, independent of the personalized form it takes. These abstract terms recall Plato, but Deleuze and Guattari refute his eternal World of Forms when they present affect as an 'entity [that] does not exist independently of something which expresses it, although it is completely distinct from it' (Deleuze and Guattari, 1988: 97). Deleuze and Guattari identify two 'poles' of the facial spectrum. The intensive face is more fluid. It expresses 'pure Power' in its extensive connections with environmental others in 'a series that makes us pass from one quality to another' (Deleuze and Guattari, 1988: 90). The reflective face expresses 'pure Quality' common to 'objects of different natures' and is of a more contemplative, thoughtful nature (Deleuze and Guattari, 1988: 90).

The cinematic face

Not only is the face a white screen reflecting back projected social meaning, it is also the 'black hole' of subjective consciousness as we engage with projected images and sounds. Yet, schizoanalysis enables us to share the camera's autonomous gaze, as a desubjectified and desubjectifying machine too. Most films still retain 'realistic' forms of photographic portraiture. Yet fantasy genres such as sci-fi and horror, with their thematic interest in human mutation, offer special modes of faciality that elude the white wall black/hole dyad to dismantle the face in startling ways. Increasingly sophisticated computer animation adds further machinic variants to these effects. Although it does not focus on cinema, the schizoanalytical model of the face uses the techniques and effects of close-up as its basis. By the magnifying properties of close-up, the face's shapes, textures and muscular movements reveal interrelated modalities. These interact intensively among themselves or extensively with other intercut close-ups, as an internal composition of close-ups in framing and montage.

A Thousand Plateaus compares the 'white wall/black hole' to the topography of a landscape with potential for deterritorialization. Hence, it becomes 'a surface: facial traits, lines, wrinkles; long face, square face, triangular face; the face is a map' (Deleuze and Guattari, 1988: 170). As 'alien landscape' *par excellence*, the cinematic face interrogates the varying nature and location of subjective identity. In close-up, it suspends individuation and attains a trans-personal quality. As a BwO, faciality can extend to a nonfacial human attribute or an inanimate object 'not because it resembles a face, but because it is imbricated in the white wall/black hole process, because it connects to the abstract machine of facialization' (Deleuze and Guattari, 1988: 175). Deleuze and Guattari assert the need to 'escape the face, to dismantle the face and facializations, to become imperceptible, to become clandestine' (Deleuze and Guattari, 1988: 171). Drugs offer one such 'clandestine' escape route and 'experimentation with drugs has left its mark on everyone, even nonusers' via art (Deleuze and Guattari, 1988: 248). They reference narcotically inspired writers and artists such as Carlos Castenada and André Michaux, but surprisingly do not extend their analysis to film. Yet, cinema's display of narcotics effects offers us startling ways to 'get off your face'.

Deleuze and Guattari extend and supplement schizoanalysis by 'pharmacoanalysis', a provocative concept that reveals the impact of drug-related art on their project (Deleuze and Guattari, 1988: 283). The term does not refer to particular drugs, or even to drugs *per se*, because 'many things can be drugs' (Deleuze and Guattari, 1988: 227). Pharmacoanalysis, rather, articulates a broader molecular perception permeated with desire. In the mescaline-driven automatic art of Micheaux, Deleuze and Guattari discover 'a whole rhizomatic perception, the moment when desire and perception meld' to manifest the imperceptible (Deleuze and Guattari, 1988: 283). Drugs in art are one way to give the unconscious the affective 'immanence and the plane that psychoanalysis has continually botched' by Oedipal fixations (Deleuze and Guattari, 1984: 284). To illustrate how facial schizo-analysis can work I explore the unnerving facial machine of *A Scanner Darkly*. The film alters faces by interpolated rotoscoping as computer animators trace live action movement frame by frame.

'Let's hear it for the Vague Blur': *A Scanner Darkly*

We have seen how for Deleuze and Guattari the face is the site of socially projected identity. On-screen faces might appear to fix this identity more firmly in close-up, but they are also potentially the film's main sites of schizo deterritorialization. Faces play a crucial role in Linklater's film and a set of facial close-ups framed by scanners even dominates the promotional graphics. The live actors were directed to exaggerate their bodily and facial movements in a cartoon-like way, enhanced by the bold strokes and emphatic movements of the artists' animations. In the titles sequence, the facial grimaces of 'D' junkie Freck (Rory Cochrane) infested by imaginary aphids in his 'garden variety psychosis' are overblown to comic effect. Later Freck overdoses and is stuck in an endless reading of his own sins by a judg-mental 'creature from between the dimensions', with a multiplicity of eyes.

Not all drug-induced affects produce such extreme facial distortions. Drug users Bob Arctor/Fred (Keanu Reeves) and Donna/Hank (Winona Rider) smoke cannabis together. Their facial outlines blur as they bliss out, getting high as a surrogate for sex and an escape from responsibility. Yet the film's most inventive cinematic device and the most suggestive tool for schizoanalysis apparently belongs on the side of the Law in the methods of narcotics agents.

Linklater's film adapts Dick's schizophrenic theme by centralizing the device of the scramble suit. According to Dick, this disguise, worn by under-cover agents consists of

a multifaceted quartz lens hooked up to a million and a half physiog-nomic fraction-representations of various people: men and women, children, with every variant encoded and then projected outward in all directions equally onto a superthin shroudlike membrane. (Dick, 1999: 16)

The computer projects an endless stream of facial features, varying age, gender and ethnicity. The film's MC at the anti-drugs meeting of the Brown Bear Lodge tells his audience that the morphing Fred is the 'ultimate Everyman', who eludes linguistic signification to make any description of him (or her) meaningless. The opening long shot of the meeting features a crowd whose faces literalize Deleuzian black holes/white walls as mere outline sketches with dot eyes and line mouths prior to individuation. This suit's scrambled face is expressed and perceived as a rapidly shifting map, briefly meshing skin tones, bone structures, hair and other features before moving into its next hybrid. Identity is radically destabilized and a perverse kind of BwO emerges as facial overload induces a becoming-imperceptible. Usually in film, tracking into close-up clarifies a character's identity. Here, however, Fred's 'vague blur' (in the MC's patronizing pleasantry) becomes more rather than less confusing when this camera movement happens. Yet, using a stable body outline as the 'screen' for live-action projections also limits their scope. Scramble-suit faces are superimposed in a hypnotic shimmer that confounds recognition. As the MC comments, 'you can barely see this man'. It is impossible to grasp these shifting identities unless the freeze-frame button on the DVD player is used to artificially still their fluctuating details. At any given moment, one eye may be brown, the other, blue, with a young woman's round chin on one side and a grizzled half beard on the other. Bone structure melts into new formations, crows-feet wrinkles appear and instantly vanish. This fluctuating blur eludes the 'latest developments in voice and facial recognition technology'.

This 'constantly shifting' defamiliarized face is a Deleuze–Guattarian facial map with the unfolding contours and colours. Linklater's visualization retains a degree of consistency in its predominant expressions ranging from neutral to emotionally intense. Multiple identities are animated over the facial movements of the actor, orchestrated rhythmically to produce multiplicity. Inside the scramble suit, Fred's 'real' face wears an anguished expression and in his own voice he comments that his assumed façade is 'terrible'. The scramble suit has been cynically invented to produce false multiplicity in order to enforce conformity by punishing deviation. We cannot read these projected faces or trust their apparent signification. Yet when Fred removes the scramble suit in the locker room and his 'Bob' persona steps out, no truthful fixed identity will emerge. He remains in a schizoid condition that splits further along with the lobes of his brain as the narrative progresses.

The repressive social order, which both drives people to substance D *and* engineers addiction, have together wrecked his mind. The New Path rehab clinics are a front for the farming and marketing of D, encouraged and distributed by narcotics agents working as dealers. For users such as Barris, the clinics are 'a seemingly voluntary privatised gulag managed to eliminate the middlemen of public accountability and free will'. Linklater's film endorses Dick's micropolitical perspective that addicts are caught in a double bind. Their search for more dangerous forms of multiplicity has been induced by the false uniformity enforced by nightmarish levels of surveillance.

When Fred finally goes 'completely bonkers', his superior 'Hank's' scramble suited face becomes even more disturbing from the subjective camera's point of view. Hank's faces no longer conform to an organic, muscular quality. Their machinic mobility becomes overtly mechanized. Meshed with the more recognisably human, some faces slip, jump and stretch in a sickening way and their relative autonomy increases disorientation. They slide apart in Picasso-like overlay. Facial expressions become rougher and more obviously cartoon-like. Line-drawings mesh in with 'live' animation, as one face becomes a crudely sketched skull. These faces are beyond Fred's control as, impelled by powerful force of the drug, they permanently dismantle his 'own' face.

The previously hidden grey membrane screen concealing Fred and Hank's 'real' faces becomes visible. Revealed as a disguise, the scramble suit loses its seductive power and becomes more obviously frightening. By this stage, the electric machinery of Fred's brain is severely damaged and has 'maybe two brain cells left that light up . . . the rest is just short circuits and sparks'. At this point, addiction is not machinic, but mechanical as narcotic multiplicity becomes brain death.

Despite Deleuze and Guattari's advocacy of art's deterritorializing power, drug-induced insights are 'all the more artificial for being based on chemical substances, hallucinatory forms, and phantasy subjectification' (Deleuze and Guattari, 1988: 283). Apparent deterritorialization rebounds into abject reterritorialization as each benefit identified is outweighed by its harmful double, so that 'the plane itself engenders dangers of its own, by which it is dismantled at the same time that it is constructed' (Deleuze and Guattari, 1988: 285). The dangers unleashed when 'lines of flight coil and start to swirl in black holes' are harrowing (Deleuze and Guattari, 1988: 285). The molecular microperceptions opened up by drugs become overlaid by their own kind of scramblesuit in 'hallucinations, delusions, false perceptions, phantasies, or paranoid outbursts' (Deleuze and Guattari, 1988: 285).

The film's final scene leaves us with a trace of optimism. Donna/Hank is actually 'Audrey', a guerrilla double agent who by counter-espionage undermines the control system she appears to support. Risk-taking and sacrifice are advocated in the present, so that 'the people of the future' can live in a better society. This phrase intriguingly echoes Deleuze and Guattari's own optimism about the political potential of 'people to come' as-yet-faceless, and their present commitment to work for their freedom (Deleuze and Guattari, 1991: 218).

Conclusion

However schizo the cinematic face might become, it remains an image. Indeed the face in close-up is *the* primal image of affect. Facial obliteration can make us painfully aware of the fragility of our own facial features. Yet, this is the very process welcomed by Deleuze and Guattari. Their schizo-analytic study of faciality reminds us how much we misguidedly invest our faces in the social and subjective construction of identity. Dismantling the face enables breaking 'through the wall of the signifier and getting out of the black hole of subjectivity' to embrace becoming (Deleuze and Guattari, 1988: 188). Yet, for Bob in *A Scanner Darkly*, drug-induced schizophrenia means brain death. The film explores the risks of getting our faces off. While warning of the dangers of drug-induced damage, Deleuze and Guattari still advocate the need to dismantle the face by the actualizing powers of art's virtual images. We cling desperately to facialization, evading the challenge of losing face to become pre-facialized. Becoming-faceless, eluding the parameters of organization, threatens to dismantle more safely subjective and temporal structures. Faciality is pivotal to the affective impact of film images. I want to assert that popular images of being 'off your face' in cinema can, in their excess, divest the face of assumed power and express the schizoid becomings of the BwO.

Chapter 10

An Ethics of Spectatorship: Love, Death and Cinema

Patricia MacCormack

The relation between cinema and spectatorship is a love relation in which the (re)negotiation of subjectivity as a perceiving entity is central to the semiotic and ethical war waged against cinema. Spectatorship is an ethical configuration beyond the screen in the world. Any claim to know an image – its meanings and pleasures – and thus desire an image as an object makes ethics impossible. It wages war against spectatorial desire and extra-image relations. In order to end the massacre of the image we must, as Guattari and Hocquenghem urge, end the massacre of pleasure, desire and the body.

Massacre occurs through signification that perceives in order to read and read in order to know: 'Here we find people preparing a great uprising of life against all the manifestations of death which continually insinuate themselves into our body, even more subtly binding our energies, reality, desire to the imperatives of the established order' (Hocquenghem, 1981: 261). The screen forms a mucosal connective tissue with our own bodies, and 'we can no longer allow others to turn our mucous membranes, our skin, all our sensitive areas into occupied territories' (Guattari, 1996: 31). Just as our bodies are occupied, so too are images, through the regimentation of desire and pleasure. Occupation results in ubiquitous death, of the subject, facilitators of desire and relations of alterity. Revolutionary thought toward ecosophy according to Guattari (2000) involves the three registers of environment, social relations and the most important, human subjectivity. Desire is the force which works through all three. 'I love you' represents the signifying chain par excellence. It is causal, the predicate is in the subject, the unfurling is narrative and logical. The 'you' is mobile, the 'I' (be it image or other sentient entity) guarantees it will always already be perceptible and thus pre-perceived. 'I oppress myself because this "I" is a product of a system of oppression' (Hocquenghem, 1981: 260). The way the 'I' perceives 'it' constitutes the 'I'. When the 'I' and 'you' are gone, and the in-between, hybrid relational is the event of ethics, where is love?

Cinema spectatorship offers revolution in signifying practices of self, world and desire, because it both shows what cannot be connected to the world in reality and relies emphatically on signifying systems for its creation and apprehension. Love for cinema is revolutionary to the extent we love the images but not the system. Signification is not exhaustive. Desire, pleasure and images are excessive, thus the turn from an analysis of the psyche toward schizoanalysis exploits 'madness [as] an excess of subjectivity' (Canguilhem, 1991: 71). Desire is found through an end to the notion of the human both as spectator and in the world constructed through a signified subject in relation to an object. We are gracious to cinema to the extent that we open up to the potentialities of thought without a compulsion to convert images to meaning for knowledge. Love is the encounter between desire and grace. As Buchanan invokes in the introduction to this volume, thought and creativity come from love for cinema. An ethics of spectatorship ends the war of signification and shifts cinematic pleasure from a situation of death to an act of love.

Analysis comes from the spectator's desire to perceive as reflection images, forms and functions and the analysis of the spectator's pleasures and desire. More precisely it comes from the spectator's perception of what appears to be within the image and the appearance of the spectator's pleasure in the world. It is a double ring of seeming. The observation of the image and the spectator are modes of analysis which, while claiming to reflect upon the image and the spectator, in fact create both. The analysis of spectatorship and cinematic pleasure are extracted from love for cinema. The double circle which orbits around the centre of the meaning-being dyad wages a war against cinematic pleasure and any possibility of thinking spectatorship as a practice of love and ethics. Knowledge wins the war before it begins. 'Dialectics is the logic of appearance. The logic of opposition is the logic of appearance . . . no one ever waged a war without having been sure of winning it' (Serres, 2007: 222–3). Perceiving meaning apprehends images before they are encountered, converting the cinematic event to pre-formed structures which constitute the possibility of perception. Perception happens before the perceptible arrives and the war is won in advance. Cinematic perception as the micro-circle which reflects the macro-circle of being perceptible makes the spectator perceptible in the world because the spectator is able to perceive. Perceptibility affirms being. The psychoanalytic shift from being perceived through the doctor-state-religious institute to perceiving oneself is seen as necessary in order to shift from sick subject, perverted or insane, to self-maintaining healthy subject. Institutes wage war on the shizo-subject, slaughtering through signification, what it means, and what Deleuze and Guattari call subjectifiation, where it is in the social order. Desire and the body are two sites of the battle-fields. The logic of appearance is always the appearance of logic and appearance as logic.

Schizoanalysis compels us toward becoming-imperceptible. Becoming-imperceptible happens when we negotiate our discrete, hermeneutic, dividuated self and emerge through our manifold relations between subjects and political spheres. We are not invisible but relational with the many and thus never alone. Guattari's work on ecosophy as a philosophy of multiple relations emphasizes as the most important element toward ethics the renegotiation of subjectivity. Ecosophy describes a terrain, dialectics a termination. Revolution according to Guattari comes from renegotiating the three ecologies of environment, human subjectivity and social relations. It is easy to see these in operation through spectatorship – the environment of the image-spectator encounter, the spectator as a desiring subject and the relation between the image and spectator as a decision toward open-ness and grace or reification of subject and object through perception via pre-formed signification. Grace is the expression of openness which cannot know the effects of opening and which offers the self as available for an encounter of becoming with an element which is not knowable and hence not necessarily desirable. Grace is found in the opening to relations, love the relation itself for an irredeemably inapprehensible other.

Death

Dialectics is death. The perceiver wages a war against all possibility of appre-hension without knowledge. The relation between elements is one of slaughter through assimilation or repudiation. Signifiers are corpses because they have already terminated any possibility of creativity or new relations. The subject in dialectics is affirmed through its dominant rela-tion and feeding off a subjugated term, and it takes without giving. Because its body is slaughtered through signification which also constructs the pos-sibility of how and what to desire the dialectic subject is the corpse-corp, of the zombie army which slaughters through conversion to meaning-knowledge. 'The always already is only a cemetery where entropy rots matter away' (Serres, 2007: 122). Through becomings and creating bodies without organs the future is opened because the present is unthought – not the yet to be thought, but the unthinkable inconvertible yet nonetheless sensible. Negotiating the sensible without conversion is an ethical turn as it makes the subject accountable for what it does with what it senses. Accountability is not deferred to a higher order, 'which means that an act is bad whenever it directly decomposes a relation, whereas it is good whenever it directly compounds its relation with other relations' (Deleuze, 1988: 35). A relation of equivalence is no relation at all. To perceive on one set of terms decomposes the relation by slaughtering the other or making it the same as the signifier-corpse. A bad relation is a relation of one toward, or *over* another, a compounding relation that proliferates trajectories to both alter the nature of the relational terms and create opportunities for other unpredictable relations.

Deleuze points out that an ethics based on obligation is bad ethics because it constructs the other as they would be judged by God, what Spinoza would call morality. Ethics is qualitative, morality a system (1988: 23). Obligation needs knowledge of another in order to be obliged. We cannot properly be obliged to a quality unless the other is perceived to 'have' that quality. Perception is limited to larger or smaller molar objects not affective intensities with which we enter into becomings. As Artaud and Deleuze and Guattari urge, we must be done with the judgement of God. What is judgement? In order to judge we must perceive and in order to perceive have a knowledge of the possibility of the perceptible. Deleuze and Guattari claim the creation of a Body without Organs confounds the judgement of God because the flesh is no longer organized into molar parts available for perception. At its most simple definition 'the body without organs is the body without an image' (Deleuze and Guattari, 1996: 8). Any perceptible elements can constitute bodies with which we make connections, so all expressions are bodies as they shift from perception as signifying to affecting-relation. When organs are molar and organized we can evaluate their function and meaning, what they can and should do. Killing God, just like Oedipus killing Laertes, is killing a dead man, a war against other corpses.

We must believe in order to kill. All perception creates belief in a thing as it converts that thing into a pre-believed. 'Consequently' write Deleuze and Guattari, '[decoding through perception and vice versa] implies a system of collective appraisal and evaluation, and a set of organs of perception, or more precisely of belief as a condition of existence and survival of the society in question' (1996: 248). The question is not what we believe, which is always measured on what we judge to be possible, but how, or that, we judge. Belief in cinema as realistic or unrealistic is irrelevant. Spectatorship is not a structure but an event with certain functional properties which are more and less affective of extra-cinematic events. Indeed believing cinema does not matter because it is not real turns away from the ethics of acknowledging all relations affect each other. Each relation is not a discrete object but traverses other relations, so thinking cinema as real is vital in reconfiguring subjectivity and modes of sensation-perception in our apprehension of the world from belief and judgement to creativity, imagination and ultimately love.

The first reorganized organ is, seemingly obviously, the eye. As the primary organ of perception of cinema (not entirely so, but it usually subjugates the ear and the nerves) the eye is seen to see. Like the seeing spectator and the spectator perceived as seeing the eye is judged based on its capacity to see. Narratively the brain perceives before the eye sees, just as the subject is perceived before images can be enjoyed appropriately. So the eye is known to know. Seeing is believing, is judging, is waging war and slaughtering, making the image a corpse and the screen a cemetery battlefield. Therefore, as Serres states 'the eye is in the tomb' (2007: 214). Serres urges us to quasi-blindness, Artaud to gaze upon the black sun, the reviled invisible but nonetheless sensed which God reviles (Artaud, 1988: 562). Spectator bodies without organs continue to 'see' with the 'eye' but the signification of sight alters and so does the meaning of the organ. We do not necessarily need to do anything as radical as sing with our sinuses, as Deleuze and Guattari encourage (Deleuze and Guattari, 1987: 151). Against their repudiation of seeing with eyes we can still use the eye for visual sensation if the structure or judgement of sight and eyes are done away with. Seeing without perceiving means the eye is not an eye. Sight is thus an act of creation. The spectator becomes the philosopher. Meaning is not closed off and effect not presumed. The affective qualities consist of the possible-perceived, what the images might create and have created with us. Additionally their effects exceed us as our capacity to sense exceeds them.

To be affected relationally by the qualities rather than value of the other, that is, to allow the other to live, constructs perception not as apprehension through evaluation but as imagination. Evaluation is always in relation to a higher and established structure, one in which the subject positions itself and thus the relation to the other is uneven, a war one has to win because the higher striated element will get to signify the lower. Whoever perceives constructs the perceptible. The perceived other is then, through a system of equivalence, allowed to come into being through the order of death, or prohibited because the equivalence is aberrant or ambiguous. Deleuze and Guattari see the system of prohibited equivalence most at work in religious structures (Deleuze and Guattari, 1999: 89–90). Science and psychiatry would incorporate these aberrations as awaiting assimilation through cure. Again however, knowledge is directly associated with slaughter, be it through prohibition or assimilation. Imagination allows a variety of ethical possibilities. One is the possibility to be wrong, or, more so, to navigate the other in a way that may not work and thus can be altered at each turn, a navigation of becoming, hybrid because it is between the two rather than comparative. Incommensurability, of languages of pleasure and perception, rather than being a failure, form a creative hybrid. The other is the possibility of fluid intensifications of power. While both elements exert and are affected by each others' powers, certain instances will see one more affected than another. Openness to be affected and that of affecting are both power qualities which mediate and oscillate the relation. The two entities are singular powers in one hybrid relation. The corpse, signified and sewn-up before it exists, no longer slaughters the other element by disallowing it to exist unless on the corpses' terms. The war of signification is fought by corpses but if the victims do not allow themselves to be buried in the cemetery they never come into being.

Imagination is mobile and plastic creation of the self and other as an in between. The subject cannot observe and is always involuted or folded as the structure itself. Knowledge and signification extricate the observing subject from the structure while simultaneously allowing the subject to create the conditions of that structure and the subject comes into being by inserting itself into the structure. The narrative goes from knowing a thing to judging the thing and then comparing the thing to self. This is the traditional narrative of cinematic perception and also of subjectivity within the world. 'The order of reasons is repetitive. The knowledge linked up in this way, infinitely iterative, is a science of death . . . Then Mars rules the world. He cuts the bodies into atomised pieces and lets them fall. This is the *foedus fati*' (Serres, 2000: 109). Thus we can see that the Order of Death, the wages of war, come not from whether we are in a social situation as opposed to a cinematic phantasy situation but what modes of knowledge, thought and perception construct ourselves and the world. The affects we do not perceive point to the imperceptible self who we are. As dialectic spectators we are human organized bodies. Many philosophers have pointed out that great art makes us inhuman. Without perceptible self we cannot perceive object outside self to our subject and dialectics are impossible. However everything else is possible so all encounters become pure possibility. The breakdown between being human and everything else is the horizon from dialectics to ecosophy.

Love

The shift from death to love emerges as the shift from perception as obligation, judgement and thus filiation with spectator, seeing as administering, to forming hybrid relations and creating unnatural offspring – future sense-perceptions as potentialities. The unnatural refers to the new natural contract where natural is no longer a category defined by the human to derogate that which challenges the primacy of the human. Only when nature is understood as everything else but and which does not sustain the category of human can we speak of the unnatural. Serres, Guattari and Deleuze urge the formation of relations with nature as a direct result of the dehumanization of the majoritarian par excellence of anthropomorphic human subjectivity and classification, perception and judgement. Deleuze and Guattari state: 'Unnatural participations or nuptials are the true Nature spanning the kingdoms of nature' (1987: 241). War is waged by humans because signifying systems creates what it means to be human. Love comes from becomings and hybridity, contracts with nature. For the spectator, an unnatural relationship with images occurs as cinema makes unnatural relations with the 'real' world. Both are actualized through each other but each are of a different kind.

'The theory of knowledge is isomorphic with that of being' writes Serres, 'let us sacrifice to Venus. The text on perception ends with conception' (2000: 39). When perception ends, knowledge of things and thus us is sacrificed to Venus, a death which slaughters the already-cadaver toward becomings. To be anew we must make pacts and participations with something else, unthought, sensible but imperceptible. *Foedera fati* performs a two-fold relation. First it attempts to ablate nature by rewriting it through linguistic systems of perception. Secondly it repudiates the effects of this ablation, the elements of nature which exceed and cannot be controlled by signifying systems and the fact that no matter how adamant those systems are, nature does respond and affect actual conditions of existence. The effluvia of human systems returns to nature, so those unexpected responses are evidence that our relation with nature is always responsive no matter how unidirectional we perceive it to be. 'Nature [is] a process of production' (Deleuze and Guattari, 1996: 3). Nature is not everything outside the human but the system by which all elements, singularities and the molecular configuration of singularities are positioned in relation with each other. Nature is nothing more than a system of non-hierarchical, non-causal and infinite relations. Deleuze and Guattari see the shift from capitalist processes to processes with and as nature involving us in a falling in love with everything because we exist in a relation of fluidity.

Love is when boundaries cannot be perceived but other elements sensed, as other elements sense us, including the elements within ourselves and that we are when becoming molecular. Our fluidity makes the demarcation with other elements impossible, molecules which are part of us are no longer our own and we must take responsibility for those molecules not from us with which we now mix. The shift to fluidity alters the terrain of perception from one of war to one of love. Relations shift from the order of Mars – *foedera fati* – to the order of Venus – *foedera naturae*. The creation of a *foedera naturae* expects and acknowledges effects of nature and forms relations which are most likely to imagine and produce beneficial affects. Production is consistent in the ethics of Spinoza, Guattari, Deleuze and Serres (among others). Production is the natural contract, which is the creation of a fluid relation between two elements which, in the *foedera fati* would be considered unnatural. One element must be slaughtered, or the relation produces – affects, new elements which are hybrid, just as the two initial elements create a hybrid mode of production, production unable to reproduce, that is, to represent. Production-relation not only produces new affects but also changes the nature of the initial elements. When we apprehend without perception we must form an unnatural participation with an image, a hybrid aesthetic encounter. Representation belongs to the *foedera fati*, production to the *foedera naturae*.

How can we think the spectator's relation with the image as a natural contract? The spectator cannot be Oedipalized because the screen will not love back. The natural contract between screen and spectator forms an ecosophical territory where our force to love – desire – cannot reproduce through a demand for reciprocation that gives us back (both produces and returns) our 'I' as human. Desire as force-production is without object and aim. In natural contracts we desire with and through proliferating elements including those within ourselves which escape us. Without reciprocated desire we cannot be objects and thus the object-subject eternal return is defunct. Deleuze and Guattari's call to becomings involve, according to anthropomorphic humanization, entities formerly perceived as devolutionary elements with which we form relations – women, animals, vegetation. They see anthropomorphism as correlative with phallocentrism, the constitutive system of desire. Facial machines and object desiring dialectics are some of the patterns of anthropomorphism we see in cinema. The organized majoritarian is not anthropomorphic in form but anthropomorphizing as system. While it is difficult to think a becoming-dog through cinema beyond representations of werewolves and other demonic on-screen pacts, what devolutionary becomings do offer are opportunities to think relations which disorganize modes of perception, just as becomings force a deconstructed perception of the humans' self. The wolf of becoming does not matter as much as what happens to our subjectivity when we howl or shiver or pack.

The question we must ask is what asignifying elements of an image – any image, it will be different for every spectator at every turn – mobilize becomings? Guattari sees any element of an image which has not yet been taken possession of by signification as a potential catalyst for becoming. Saturations of hue, sonorities, elements of art unmoored from their capacity to inform the spectator of the form and function of an image are aspects of cinema with which we enter into asemiotic participations. While Guattari suggests certain examples as more or less mobilizing, any element should not be understood as inherently asignifying, it is the spectator's responsibility, creativity and desire which apprehend images before and beyond perception as rupturing events. Ethics comes with what we produce from what we sense. Representation is reality in capitalism. Thus the reality of that 'represented' (i.e. here aesthetically created to be presented) in cinema is schizo. 'Shit on your whole mortifying imaginary, and symbolic theatre' write Deleuze and Guattari, 'what does schizoanalysis ask? Nothing more than a bit of a *relation to the outside*, a little real reality' (1996: 334). The natural contract demands relation with everything it would seem is impossible for the human to desire and with which the human can relate.

The Oedipal parents produce because they reproduce. Our demand for their love produces us. Love for the nonhuman makes us nonhuman and the love produces the unthinkable because anything produced comes outside of pre-formed symbolic. Reality, like nature, is that which in humanity would be considered unreal – images as immaterial. Covertly cinematic images are more material than subjectivity and the human world. Institutional systems of family, state and church convert, according to Guattari, the real materiality affective qualities of natural – that is, extra-human – elements, from animals and vegetal forms to art and music – to the phantasmatic theatre of signifying and signified 'life', the slaughtered life of the *foedera fati*. Guattari claims psychosis is defined institutionally as the hypnosis of the real. The psychotic perceives the very 'avoidance, displacement, misrecognition, distortion, overdetermination, ritualisation' (1995: 79) signifying systems deny is within all perception. If psychosis is what Guattari calls the hypnosis of the real, that is, conversion of the real hypnotized into a false dream-world of empty symbols and structures (which is why he claims we are all psychotic) is the shift from cinema as aesthetic to real the hypnosis of the artificial which is the symbolic? Taking cinema as real demands a schizo-spectator.

As schizo-spectators we must respond to the demand of ethics because we acknowledge that all perception is creation and all relations produce affects, be they in the cinema or world. The ordering of real/image is the same as human/everything else, both a myth that conceals its own conditions of possibility and a system that perceives through equivalence. The spectator-screen event forms a Body without Organs as an erogenous body. The erogenous body is created through 'a pure dispersed and anarchic multiplicity, without unity or totality, and whose elements are welded, pasted together by the real distinction or the very absence of a link' (Deleuze and Guattari, 1996: 324). The erogenous body is a territory of becoming through relations of desire. The only condition of this zone is that the relation must be unnatural because the singularities are inter-kingdom. Women, animals, machines, music are all singularities with which Deleuze and Guattari suggest becoming-relations. Images are infinite in the singularities they offer. Form elements can elicit becomings through unnatural gestures, angles, colour and other asignifying elements.

The spectatorial event itself, which culturally is arguably both the most natural and unnatural territory of our time, is an inter-kingdom participation. It is the world of pure possibility in that we see what we can never see in the world through both modes of perception – the extreme close up, slow motion and so on, and event-form-world – enhanced in particular genres such as fantasy and science-fiction but present nonetheless in all films. Desire through becomings turns toward the unresponsive and un-like image, unlike the world and unlike us. Ethics acknowledges that whatever an image's resonance with the world outside the screen, through all perception there is production which creates and affects our relation with all other entities. Love for that which cannot love back is Oedipally irrational. It must therefore access the unconscious by being love which cannot perceive its object, as the object must function to affirm the desiring subject. Capitalism and psychoanalysis compel love not for objects but for the very machine itself – a necrophilic love for the *foedera fati*. When the love object does not love back the territory of love changes.

Cinema is not unreal escape, it allows us to explode into the world through unnatural perception of the human via a natural contract of dissipative and asignified-asubjectified relations. 'The crucial objective is to grasp the a-signifying points of rupture – the rupture of denotation, connotation and signification – from which a certain number of semiotic chains are put to work in the service of an auto-referential effect' (Guattari, 2005: 56). In some ways cinema is an easy first step for thinking different desiring-machines in that it both does and does not constitute an object but it does proliferate particles and lines of desire through trajectories which are visible as (possibly perverse) desired forms, invisible as unmoored elements (angle, colour) and always more than we are able to perceive.

These elements are what Guattari calls the *dispositifs* of the production of subjectivity (Guattari, 1995: 34).

A spectator Body without Organs senses the image as its own Body without Organs, the consistency between them is the erogenous body of schizo-cinesexuality. To perceive is always an act of production, in representation it is reproduction. In the natural contract this is production as phylum. Perception and production are also enunciation in the affects they emit into the world they constitute. The organ-ized mouth is the speaking organ which, through representation, vomits empty symbols. 'Don't speak with your mouth full' Guattari reminds us, 'it's very bad manners!' Spectatorship is speaking with your mouth full – both ingestion and gurgitation. Speaking in tongues is present in all Deleuze and Guattari's inter-kingdom becomings, the animal howl, the woman's illogical speech, the sonority of music and colour to the imperceptible sound. Demonic speech is a multi-tongued thousand tiny utterances which both hear and speak within their singular assemblage. Schizoanalysis 'puts us in contact with the "demoniacal" element in nature' (Deleuze and Guattari, 1996: 35) as becoming-animal 'implies an initial relation of alliance with a demon' (1987: 247). The werewolf and the vampire infect through hybrid mouth encounters which produces incommensurable creative languages and modes of perception, speech that does not reproduce but produces unique polyvocal language. All of these are nonhuman, non-anthropomorphic, nonsensical speeches made from perceptions unable to be converted to signs.

To speak with our mouths full is to receive polyvocally and as perception is creation to create polyvocally. 'I don't get it and so I don't like it' is a univocal enunciation of desire where one mode of speech must win the war. Similarly 'I like it because I don't get it' is transgression for its own sake which again returns and relies on the univocal expression of humanizing signification. Sight is speech, the eyes are tongues and erogenous flesh is the eyes-ears-tongues particles of perception as asemiotic sensation, knowledge as thought from the outside and enunciation as mediation. Just as the terms of becoming appear devolutionary – from woman to animal to imperceptible – so too these apprehensions of images could be constructed as failures, or schiz-fluxes of madness. The most difficult question is how do we create desiring machines from and between the schiz-machine of cinesexuality and the political socius? Where does schiz-spectatorship traverse schiz-politics? The ecologies are not discrete. Ethics is traversal, which according to humanism would be unnatural. Inter-kingdom traversals relate cinematic encounter with world encounter, subjectivity as always constituted by regulated and ubiquitous modes of perception, contextualized but not necessarily apprehended differently between environments, and relations of alterity between subjects, modes of perception and accountable affectivity.

An ethics of spectatorship remains cinematic and is not cinematic at once. Cinematic ethics comes from traversal. Just as becomings traverse kingdoms, so cinematic ethics traverses the false dichotomies set up by signifying systems – sensation/perception, real/unreal, aesthetic/political and so forth. The territories of cinema and socius are manufactured as different but both operate under the same semiotic chain. To love an image is to allow both vocalities of image and spectator to exist simultaneously, creating speech which is chaotic but not irredeemably so. The seemingly paradoxical question is how we listen to the many foreign tongues within the one plane while being aware cinema and society work upon a homogenous plane of signification? 'Schizo chaosmosis is a means for the appearance of abstract machines which work traversally to heterogenous strata' (Guattari, 1995: 82–3). It may be that we are more likely to find revolutionary dissipations of desire through spectatorship precisely because we initially define our situation of sensation-perception as spectators as markedly different to those of the world outside of cinema. Spectatorship through asemiosis slaughters majoritarianism and thus involves risk, a 'fearsome involution calling us toward unheard of becomings' (Deleuze and Guattari, 1987: 240). The primary line of traversal is desire and the ethical affect is perception. Because cinema does not love back the demand for grace toward the infinite other – other entity but also other particle or intensity – is easily transcribed to the non-cinematic world.

Grace accepts that to not understand does not mean nothing is produced, and the other may never respond to us, thus never be an object which knows us and affirm our knowledge of our subjective self. There is a turn away which slaughters by refusing to sense and a turn toward which faces the risks and pleasures of indifferent affectivity that produces beyond the cinematic encounter whether it is perceived or not. The extent to which we are gracious to this encounter informs the revolutions cinematic perception can invoke transversally. Guattari claims through chaosophy we operate like artists rather than scientists and politicians (Guattari, 2005: 35). The spectator creates the work of art as inter-affective encounter. Art exploits the chaos which is always the nature of things upon which homogenous signifying systems impose themselves. Artistic configurations of chaos create new territories which traverse the limits of what is art and what is not. If art makes us inhuman it must encourage us to form natural contracts in unnatural alliances. Art itself creates unnatural alliances in order to shift from the logical and true to the reterritorializing and contingent – neither true nor false but measured on what is produced. The world thus becomes art as we acknowledge our creation of it, and art, as the extent to which we show grace to our artistic territories of desire, here the screen-spectator relation as a natural contract, a *foedera naturae*, a relation of love.

Notes

Introduction

[1] In the past, I have used the word 'dialectical' to describe essentially the same reading attitude. See Buchanan, 2000.

[2] In a different place, I have shown how this dualism operates in Deleuze's thought on music. See Buchanan, 2000: 175–89.

[3] Virilio (1994: 14) suggests that both photography and cinema learnt a great deal about the essential nature of the image from pioneering work in animal conditioning done in the 1920s and 1930s.

[4] For an excellent explanation of the concept of spiritual automaton and its significance to Deleuze's work on cinema, see Rodowick, 1997: 174–7.

[5] I have developed this point at greater length in Buchanan, 2007.

[6] Here I equate the repetition of a certain way of making films with 'method', about which Deleuze says the following: 'Method is the means of that knowledge which regulates the collaboration of all the faculties. It is therefore the manifestation of common sense or the realisation of a *Cogitatio natura*, and presupposes a good will as though this were a "premeditated decision" of the thinker' (Deleuze, 1994: 165). The significance of this, as should become clear in what follows, is that in Deleuze's view the application of method is a sure-fire way of stifling creativity and with it the production of thought. Deleuze's (1986: 155–9) remarks on the Actor's Studio are instructive in this regard because he argues that their famous method style of acting was employed precisely to escape the limitations of the sensory-motor scheme in which it was formed.

[7] I take the idea of 'image-regimes' from Rodowick, 2001: 170–7. I have explored the connection between 'image-regime' and the 'regime of signs' in more detail in Buchanan, 2007.

[8] For a more detailed discussion of this point see Buchanan, 2007. It is perhaps worth adding at this point that Virilio, too, is a keen observer of the delirious qualities and powers of the image's distortion of both dimension and proportion. See Virilio, 1989: 25.

[9] 'In thinking we obey only the laws of thought, laws that determine both the form and the content of true ideas, and that make us produce ideas in sequence according to their own causes and through our own power, so that in knowing our power of understanding we know through their causes all the things that fall within this power' (Deleuze, 1990: 140).

[10] In a different place, I have tried to show that Deleuze's oeuvre as a whole is motivated by this dialectic between sad passions and adequate ideas. See Buchanan, 2000.

[11] I develop this notion of the plane of self-evidence or plane of obviousness in Buchanan, 2008.

[12] To give only one example, its appeal to teenage boys is why the *X-men* trilogy got made and Kim Stanley Robinson's more cerebral *Mars* trilogy didn't, even though the rights to it have been optioned by James Cameron, who as the director of *Terminator* and *Titanic* has obvious money-making credentials.

[13] Not even sophisticated versions of market analysis such as Franco Moretti's (2001) cultural geography, which uses sales data to chart patterns in national taste, explain *why* desire manifests itself in the way it does, nor *why* it is distributed in the way it is.

Chapter 3

[1] Deleuze and Guattari capitalize 'Other Person' (*Autri*) once they construct it as a concept in order to distinguish it from other versions of the same concept.

[2] Deleuze discusses the problem of the Other Person in *Difference and Repetition*, where he writes: 'Even Sartre was content to inscribe this oscillation in the other as such, in showing that the other became object when I became subject, and did not become subject unless I in turn became object. As a result, the structure of the other, as well as its role in psychic systems, remained misunderstood' (1994: 260).

Chapter 4

[1] Brian Massumi notes in *A User Guide to Capitalism and Schizophrenia* that 'Filmmakers and painters are philosophical thinkers to the extent that they explore the potentials of their respective mediums *and break away from the beaten paths*' (Massumi, 1992: 6, my emphasis).

[2] The character of the Stalker orients himself in the zone by the dispersal of weighted threads, which he throws ahead and horizontally to ensure safe passage. The threads are used to determine a safe passage into and out of the zone. This indicates that the patterns of potential safe routes by which one may navigate the zone are unpredictable and open to constant variation and always means moving forward. The threads are retrieved only to precipitate further forward motion. The contribution of what has passed into virtuality alleviates not only the actuality of the moment of decision, but also what is immanent by recognition of its inconsistency – the anxiety that no expectations can be fulfilled in mere reflection and certainty that in the way forward one cannot necessarily find comfort and assurance in what has gone before. When Deleuze and Guattari propose a positive deterritorialization that is essentially creative, they suggest that philosophical, artistic and scientific creation offer new lines of thought through the realization of 'abstract machines' and 'diagrams'.

[3] Deleuze and Guattari's view of capitalism (in derritorialization guise) is that it sets adrift schizophrenic fluxes of bits, scraps of things, people, words, customs and beliefs which it then reterritorializes in the Oedipal family.

[4] Kelvin argues: 'the cell and the nucleus of the cell are nothing but camouflage. The real structure, which determines the functions of the visitor, remains

concealed' (Lem, 2003: 106). Bogue notes that the implication of consciousness as dynamism can be interpreted at a subatomic level through differentiation of velocity and degrees (the size of interval) and based in the complexity of any event.

5 She has the mark of the fatal injection on her arm (a key moment in the narrative of both novel and film is Kelvin's recognition of Hari via the tear in her dress and the puncture wound of the hypodermic needle – visceration as the event of acknowledgement). Later when the visitor voluntarily submits herself to annihilation through sacrifice she achieves a kind of 'human stature'.

6 Deleuze interprets the subjectivity of the fragmentary vision (the crystal-image) as synonymous with European post-war cinema.

7 Bogue argues: 'an object (a merely present image) emits light and that some rays of light pass through unnoticed, while others are reflected back onto the object. Our representation of the object consists of rays of light we reflect, that is, the object's total number of rays minus the rays we ignore or do not reflect. An organ of perception functions as the mirror that reflects the rays that interest us and that serve our future actions' (31).

8 In both the film and the novel when the visitor first appears, Kelvin notices, in attempting to remove her dress (he asks her to don a spacesuit seemingly to go on a reconnaissance mission but in reality it is his first attempt to rid himself of the visitor) that there are no fastenings. This implies that Solaris, in reading his memory, has been selective (the visitor is not a complete facsimile).

9 The interruptive aspect of undifferentiated amorality has a strong parallel in *Stalker*. The reading of Kelvin's memory by the ocean to facilitate the visitor does not distinguish between good and bad memory. The room in *Stalker* also does not fulfil merely conscious desire but grants and interprets the unconscious wish regardless of the repercussions to the wisher maker.

10 During the traversal of the zone, the three travellers discuss the demise of another stalker (Porcupine) who entered 'the room' and was seemingly granted his wish. On his return he inexplicably became wealthy but within a week had committed suicide. The implication is that the room does not read and act upon the superficiality of any surface desire but rather delves deeper and interprets darker unconscious wishes.

11 Deleuze and Guattari note in *A Thousand Plateaus* that 'The ambiguity of the "far-seers" situation is that they are able to detect the slightest microinfraction in the abyss, things the others do not see . . .' (Deleuze and Guattari, 1996: 202).

12 Deleuze and Guattari go on to say that 'All faces envelop an unknown, unexplored landscape; all landscapes are populated by a loved or dreamed-of face, develop a face to come or already past. What face has not called upon the landscapes it amalgamated, sea and hill; what landscape has not evoked the face that would have completed it, providing an unexpected complement for its lines or traits?' (Deleuze and Guattari, 1996: 172–3).

13 The novel, written by the Strugatsky brothers, is entitled *Roadside Picnic* and is so named to suggest the temporary incursion of aliens thirty years prior to the commencement of the narrative and who picnicked on earth and left leaving a series of locations permanently contaminated by their debris. In the novel this residue is very real and the source of an underground economy for stalkers.

In Tarkovsky's film, what is desired is wish fulfilment from the room. However, it appears to grant the truth of the deeper self and not the apparent reality of the surface self.

[14] Tarkovsky expands this idea of the 'miracle' by suggesting at the end of the film that Monkey has telepathic powers. In a sequence which mirrors the opening shot of the film, objects move across a surface in the stalker's apartment as the result of the vibration of a passing train. In the final sequence Monkey appears to be watching a similar event, but it is only after the train has passed that we are aware that the objects continue to move and that Monkey is manipulating them.

Chapter 5

[1] Bergman, *Cahiers du Cinema*, October 1959, cited in Deleuze (1986: 99).

[2] Deleuze and Guattari, drawing on Pierre Klossowski, point to an analogous, deterritorializing potential in science (1983: 367–72).

[3] For a cogent description of these tasks in relation to literature and the arts, see Stivale, 1980.

[4] Deleuze's description of the cinematic face is strikingly similar to that of the plateau, 'a continuous, self-vibrating region of intensities whose development avoids any orientation toward a culmination point or external end' (Deleuze and Guattari, 1987: 22).

[5] Rushton (2002) provides an illuminating discussion of Deleuze's work on the face in relation to virtuality and the possible.

[6] Ronald Bogue (2003: 95–105) presents a detailed reading of this plateau in relation to Jean Paris's *L'Espace et le regard*, which outlines the evolution of the gaze as represented in Western art, and appears to have guided Deleuze and Guattari's thinking. Duccio, Giotto and the Byzantine icon figure prominently in both texts.

[7] See Patricia MacCormack (2004) for a compelling reading of the probe-head in relation to the contemporary Australian queer performance artist Pluto.

[8] The plateau on faciality is further peppered with references to close-ups in films, particularly the close-ups from G. W. Pabst's *Pandora's Box* (1928) of the faces of Lulu, Jack the Ripper, and the knife that are central to Deleuze's discussion of the cinematic affection-image.

[9] Director's commentary, *Bad Education* (2005), dir. Pedro Almodóvar [DVD], United States: Sony Pictures Home Entertainment.

Chapter 7

[1] For a more detailed account of recent Quebec cinema, see Marshall, 2005.

[2] Robert Schwartzwald's (1991) critique of Thérien is apposite to the point I'm making here.

Chapter 8

1 Here an interesting comparison could be made to the function of the tape-recorder in the consulting-room of the psychoanalyst, discussed by Deleuze and Guattari in *Anti-Oedipus*: 'Leave your desiring-machines at the door, give up your orphan and celibate machines, your tape-recorder and your little bike, enter and allow yourself to be oedipalized' (Deleuze and Guattari, 1983: 58). The introduction of the tape-recorder ('after a schizophrenic flash') is a breaking of the Oedipal contract. In *Alienations* we see that the camera is not necessarily an intrusion into the Oedipal secret that releases schizoid flows of desire, but a desiring-machine that also releases Oedipal traumas.

2 For an elaboration on the changes of the family in migration and in media practices, see Pisters and Staat, 2005.

3 See also Martin-Jones (2006) and Pisters (2006) on the connections between movement- and time-images.

4 See also Linda Williams's (1989) historical analysis of cinema as belonging to this paradigm, connecting it to the nineteenth century's 'frenzy of the visible'.

5 Deleuze calls this belief 'the subtle way out': To believe, not in a different world, but in a link between man and the world, in love or life, to believe in this as the impossible, the unthinkable, which none-the-less cannot but be thought: 'something possible or I will suffocate'. 'It is this belief that makes the unthought the specific power of thought, through the absurd, by virtue of the absurd' (Deleuze, 1989: 170).

Bibliography

Introduction

Badiou, A. (2006), *Polemics*, trans. S. Corcoran, London: Verso.

Badiou, A. (2005), *Infinite Thought: Truth and the Return of Philosophy*, trans. O. Feltham and J. Clemens, London: Continuum.

Baudrillard, J. (1996), *The System of Objects*, trans. J. Benedict, London: Verso.

Benjamin, W. (1973), *Charles Baudelaire: A Lyric Poet in the Era of High Capitalism*, trans. H. Zohn, London: Verso.

Benjamin, W. (1968), 'The work of art in the age of mechanical reproduction', in H. Arendt (ed.), *Illuminations*, trans. H. Zohn, New York: Schocken Books, pp. 217–51.

Buchanan, I. (2008), *Deleuze and Guattari's Anti-Oedipus*, London: Continuum.

Buchanan, I. (2007), 'Is a schizoanalysis of cinema possible?', *Cinémas: Revue d'études cinématographiques*, 16 (2–3), 117–45.

Buchanan, I. (2000), *Deleuzism: A Metacommentary*, Durham, NC: Duke University Press.

Deleuze, G. and Guattari, F. (1994), *What Is Philosophy?*, trans. H. Tomlinson and G. Burchell, New York: Columbia University Press.

DeLanda, M. (2006), *A New Philosophy of Society: Assemblage Theory and Social Complexity*, London: Continuum.

Deleuze, G. (2006), *Two Regimes of Madness: Texts and Interviews 1975–1995*, in D. Lapoujade (ed.), trans. A. Hodges and M. Taormina, New York: Semiotext(e).

Deleuze, G. and Guattari, F. (2004), *Anti-Oedipus* [New Edition], trans. R. Hurley, M. Seem and H. R. Lane, London and New York: Continuum.

Deleuze, G. (2003), *Francis Bacon: The Logic of Sensation*, trans. D. W. Smith, London: Continuum.

Deleuze, G. (1994), *Difference and Repetition*, trans. P. Patton, London: Continuum.

Deleuze, G. (1990), *The Logic of Sense*, trans. M. Lester and C. Stivale, London: Continuum.

Deleuze, G. (1989), *Cinema 2: The Time-Image* , trans. H. Tomlinson and R. Galeta, Minneapolis: University of Minnesota Press.

Deleuze, G. (1986), *Cinema 1: The Movement-Image*, trans. H. Tomlinson and R. Galeta, Minneapolis: University of Minnesota Press.

Guattari, F. (1995a), *Chaosophy*, S. Lotringer (ed.), New York: Semiotext(e).

Guattari, F. (1995b), *Chaosmosis: An Ethico-Aesthetic Paradigm*, trans. P. Bains and J. Pefanis, Sydney: Power Institute.

Jameson, F. (2002), *A Singular Modernity: Essay on the Ontology of the Present*, London: Verso.

Metz, C. (1982), *The Imaginary Signifier: Psychoanalysis and the Cinema*, trans. C. Britton et al., Bloomington and Indianapolis: Indiana University Press.

Moretti, F. (2001), 'Planet Hollywood', *New Left Review*, 9, 90–101.

Rodowick, D. N. (2001), *Reading the Figural, or, Philosophy After New Media*, Durham: Duke University Press.
Rodowick, D. N. (1997), *Gilles Deleuze's Time Machine*, Durham : Duke University Press.
Virilio, P. (1994), *The Vision Machine*, trans. J. Rose, Bloomington and Indianapolis: Indianapolis University Press.
Virilio, P. (1989), *War and Cinema: The Logistics of Perception*, trans. P. Camiller, London: Verso.

Chapter 1

Deleuze, G. (1994), *Difference and Repetition*, trans. P. Patton, New York: Columbia University Press.
Deleuze, G. (1990), *The Logic of Sense*, trans. M. Lester and C. Stivale, New York: Columbia University Press.
Deleuze, G. (1989), *Cinema 2: The Time-Image*, trans. H. Tomlinson and R. Galeta, Minneapolis: University of Minnesota Press.
Deleuze, G. (1986), *Cinema 1: The Movement-Image*, trans. H. Tomlinson and B. Habberjam, Minneapolis: University of Minnesota Press.
Deleuze, G. and Guattari, F. (1983), *Anti-Oedipus: Capitalism and Schizophrenia*, trans. R. Hurley, M. Seem and H. R. Lane, Minneapolis: University of Minnesota Press.
Husserl, E. (2001), *Analyses Concerning Passive and Active Syntheses: Lectures on Transcendental Logic*, trans. A. Steinbock, Dordrecht: Kluwer Academic Publishers.
Kant, I. (1998), *Critique of Pure Reason*, trans. P. Guyer and A. W. Wood, New York: Cambridge University Press.
Steinbock, A. J. (2001), 'Introduction', in E. Husserl (ed.), *Analyses Concerning Passive and Active Syntheses: Lectures on Transcendental Logic*, trans. A. Steinbock. Dordrecht: Kluwer Academic Publishers, pp. i–lxvii.

Chapter 2

Deleuze, G. (2004), *Desert Islands and Other Texts: 1953–1974*, Cambridge, MA: M.I.T. Press.
Deleuze, G. (1989), *Cinema 2: The Time-Image*, London: Continuum.
Deleuze, G. and Guattari, F. (2004), *Anti-Oedipus: Capitalism and Schizophrenia*, London: Continuum.
Phillips, G. D. (ed.) (2001), *Stanley Kubrick Interviews*, Jackson: University of Mississippi Press.

Chapter 3

Deleuze, G. and Guattari, F. (1994), *What Is Philosophy?*, trans. H. Tomlinson and G. Burchell, New York: Columbia University Press.

Deleuze, G. and Guattari, F. (1987), *A Thousand Plateaus: Capitalism and Schizophrenia*, trans. B. Massumi, Minneapolis: University of Minnesota Press.

Deleuze, G. and Parnet, C. (2002), *Dialogues*, trans. H. Tomlinson, B. Habberjam and E. Albert, New York: Columbia University Press.

Deleuze, G. (2006), 'The brain is the screen', in D. Lapoujade (ed.), *Two Regimes of Madness*, trans. A. Hodges and M. Taorimina, New York: Semiotext(e), pp. 287–96.

Deleuze, G. (2001), *Cinema 1: The Movement-Image*, trans. H. Tomlinson, Minneapolis: University of Minnesota Press.

Deleuze, G. (1994), *Difference and Repetition*, trans. P. Patton, New York: Columbia University Press.

Kant, I. (1965), *Critique of Pure Reason*, trans. N. K. Smith, New York: Bedford Press.

Vermilye, J. (2002), *Ingmar Bergman: His Life and Films*, Jefferson, and New York: McFarland.

Chapter 4

Bogue, R. (2003), *Deleuze on Cinema*, London: Routledge.

Bogue, R. (1989), *Deleuze and Guattari*, London: Routledge.

Deleuze, G. (1997), *Cinema 1*, trans. H. Tomlinson and B. Habberjam, London: Continuum.

Deleuze, G. (1994), *Difference and Repetition*, trans. P. Patton. New York: Columbia University Press.

Deleuze, G. (1990), *The Logic of Sense*, trans. M. Lester and C. Stivale, London: Continuum.

Deleuze, G. (1989), *Cinema 2*, trans. H. Tomlinson and R. Galeta, Minneapolis: University of Minnesota Press.

Deleuze, G. (1983), *Nietzsche and Philosophy*, trans. H. Tomlinson, London: Continuum.

Deleuze, G. and Guattari, F. (1996), *A Thousand Plateaus/Capitalism & Schizophrenia*, trans. B. Massumi, London: Continuum.

Deleuze, G. and Guattari, F. (1994), *What Is Philosophy?*, trans. G. Burchell and H. Tomlinson, London & New York: Verso.

Deleuze, G. and Guattari, F. (1986), *Nomadology: The War Machine*, trans. B. Massumi, New York: Semiotext(e).

Deleuze, G. and Guattari, F. (1983), *Anti-Oedipus/Capitalism and Schizophrenia*, trans. R. Hurley, M. Seem and H. R. Lane, Minneapolis: University of Minnesota Press.

Flaxman, G. (2000), 'Introduction', in G. Flaxman (ed.), *The Brain Is the Screen*, Minneapolis: University of Minnesota Press, pp. 1–60.

Le Fanu, M. (1990), *The Cinema of Andrei Tarkovsky*, London: B.F.I.

Lem, S. (2003), *Solaris*, trans. J. Kilmartin and S. Cox, London: Faber and Faber.

Massumi, B. (1992), *A Users Guide to Capitalism and Schizophrenia*, Cambridge, MA: M.I.T. Press.

Rodowick, D. N. (1997), *Deleuze's Time Machine*, Durham : Duke University Press.

Strugatsky, A. and Strugatsky, B. (2000), *Roadside Picnic*, trans. A. W. Bouis, London: Victor Gollancz.

Tarkovsky, A. (1994), *Time within Time – The Diaries 1970–86*, trans. K. Hunter-Blair, London: Faber and Faber.

Tarkovsky, A. (1986), *Sculpting in Time*, trans. K. Hunter-Blair, London: Bodley Head.

Turovskaya, M. (1989), *Tarkovsky – Cinema as Poetry*, trans. N. Ward, London: Faber and Faber.

Chapter 5

Bergson, H. (1991), *Matter and Memory*, trans. N. M. Paul and W. S. Palmer, New York: Zone Books.

Bogue, R. (2003), *Deleuze on Music, Painting, and the Arts*, New York: Routledge.

Deleuze, G. (1986), *Cinema 1: The Movement-Image*, trans. H. Tomlinson and B. Habberjam, Minneapolis: University of Minnesota Press.

Deleuze, G. and Guattari, F. (1994), *What Is Philosophy?*, trans. H. Tomlinson and G. Burchell, New York: Columbia University Press.

Deleuze, G. and Guattari, F. (1987), *A Thousand Plateaus: Capitalism and Schizophrenia*, trans. B. Massumi, Minneapolis: University of Minnesota Press.

Deleuze, G. and Guattari, F. (1983), *Anti-Oedipus: Capitalism and Schizophrenia*, trans. R. Hurley, M. Seem and H. R. Lane, Minneapolis: University of Minnesota Press.

Guattari, F. (1998), 'Schizoanalysis', *Yale Journal of Criticism*, 11 (2), 433–9.

Guattari, F. (1996), *Soft Subversions*, S. Lotringer (ed.), trans. D. L. Sweet and C. Wiener, New York: Semiotext(e).

MacCormack, P. (2004), 'The probe-head and the faces of Australia: from Australia Post to Pluto', *Journal of Australian Studies*, 81, 135–225.

Rushton, R. (2002), 'What can a face do? On Deleuze and faces', *Cultural Critique*, 51 (Spring), 219–37.

Stivale, C. J. (1980), 'Gilles Deleuze & Félix Guattari: schizoanalysis & literary discourse', *SubStance*, 9 (4), 46–57.

Chapter 6

Bergson, H. (1998), *Creative Evolution*, trans. A. Mitchell, New York: Dover Publications Inc.

Bergson, H. (1988), *Matter and Memory*, trans. N. M. Paul and W. S. Palmer, New York: Zone Books.

Bogue, R. (1989), *Deleuze and Guattari*, London: Routledge.

Deleuze, G. (1989), *Cinema 2: The Time-Image*, trans. H. Tomlinson and R. Galeta, London: Continuum.

Deleuze, G. (1986), *Cinema 1: The Movement-Image*, trans. H. Tomlinson and B. Habberjam, London: Continuum.

Deleuze, G. and Guattari, F. (1987), *A Thousand Plateaus: Capitalism and Schizophrenia*, trans. B. Massumi, London: Continuum.

Deleuze, G. and Guattari, F. (1983), *Anti-Oedipus: Capitalism and Schizophrenia*, trans. R. Hurley, M. Seem and H. R. Lane, Minneapolis: University of Minnesota Press.

Eleftheriotis, D. (2001), *Popular Cinemas of Europe*, New York: Continuum.

Frayling, C. (1981), *Spaghetti Westerns*, London: I. B. Tauris.

Gunning, T. (1990), 'The cinema of attractions: early film, its spectator and the avant-garde', in T. Elsaesser (ed.), *Early Cinema: Space, Frame, Narrative*, London: British Film Institute, 56–62.

Holland, E. (1999), *Deleuze and Guattari's Anti-Oedipus: Introduction to Schizoanalysis*, London: Routledge.

Martin-Jones, D. (2006), *Deleuze, Cinema and National Identity*, Edinburgh: Edinburgh University Press.

Pisters, P. (2003), *The Matrix of Visual Culture*, Stanford: Stanford University Press.

Thomas, R. (1985), 'Indian cinema: pleasures and popularity', *Screen*, 25 (3–4), 116–31.

Wagstaff, C. (1998), 'Italian genre films in the world market', in G. N. Smith and S. Ricci (eds), *Hollywood and Europe*, London: BFI, pp. 74–85.

Wagstaff, C. (1992), 'A forkful of westerns: industry, audiences and the Italian western', in R. Dyer and G. Vincendeau (eds), *Popular European Cinema*, London: Routledge, pp. 245–61.

Chapter 7

Arcand, D. (1964), 'Cinéma et sexualité', *Parti pris*, 9–11, 90–7.

Bergstrom, J. (1979), 'Alternation, segmentation, hypnosis: interview with Raymond Bellour', *Camera Obscura*, 3–4, 71–103.

Deleuze, G. (1989), *Cinema 2: The Time Image*, trans. H. Tomlinson and R. Galeta, London: Continuum.

Deleuze, G. and Guattari, F. (1987), *A Thousand Plateaus: Capitalism and Schizophrenia*, trans. B. Massumi, London: Continuum.

Deleuze, G. and Guattari, F. (1986), *Kafka: Toward a Minor Literature*, trans. D. Polan, Minneapolis: University of Minnesota Press.

Garrity, H. (1989–90), 'Subversive discourse in Yves Simoneau's *Pouvoir intime*', *Québec Studies*, 9, 29–37.

Jameson, F. (1986), 'Third-world literature in the era of multinational capitalism', *Social Text*, 15, 65–88.

Larose, J. (1989), 'Images pressées', *Revue belge du cinéma*, 27, 25–8.

Maheu, P. (1964), 'L'Oedipe colonial', *Parti pris*, 9–11, 19–29.

Marshall, B. (2005), 'Quebec cinema 2005: reflections on a complex territory', *Vertigo*, 2 (9), 42–4.

Marshall, B. (2001), *Quebec National Cinema*. Montreal: McGill-Queen's University Press.

Schwartzwald, R. (1991), 'Fear of Federasty: Québec's inverted fictions', in H. J. Spillers (ed.), *Comparative American Identities: Race, Sex and Nationality in the Modern Text*, London: Routledge, pp. 175–95.

Thérien, G. (1987), 'Cinéma québécois: la difficile conquête de l'altérité', *Littérature*, 66, 101–14.

Weinmann, H. (1990), Cinéma de l'imaginaire québécois: de La Petite Aurore à Jésus de Montréal, Montreal: l'Hexagone.

Chapter 8

Comolli, J. (1980), 'Machines of the visible', in T. de Lauretis and S. Heath (eds), *The Cinematic Apparatus*, Houndsmills and London: MacMillan, pp. 121–42.

Deleuze, G. (2006), *Two Regimes of Madness: Texts and Interviews, 1975–1995*, trans. M. Taormina and A. Hodges, New York: Semiotexte/Foreign Agent.

Deleuze, G. (2000), 'The brain is the screen', trans. M. T. Guirgis, in G. Flaxman (ed.), *The Brain Is the Screen: Deleuze and the Philosophy of Cinema*. Minneapolis and London: University of Minnesota Press, pp. 365–74.

Deleuze, G. (1997), *Essays Critical and Clinical*, trans. D. W. Smith and M. A. Greco, Minneapolis and London: University of Minnesota Press.

Deleuze, G. (1989), *Cinema 2: The Time-Image*, trans. H. Tomlinson and R. Galeta, London: Continuum.

Deleuze, G. (1985), *Cinema 1: The Movement-Image*, trans. B. Habberjam and H. Tomlinson, London: Continuum.

Deleuze, G. and Guattari, F. (1988), *A Thousand Plateaus: Capitalism and Schizophrenia*, trans. B. Massumi, London: Continuum.

Deleuze, G. and Guattari, F. (1984), *Anti-Oedipus: Capitalism and Schizophrenia*, trans. R. Hurley, M. Seem and H. R. Lane, London: Continuum.

Friston, K. J. (1998), 'The disconnection hypothesis', *Schizophrenia Research*, 30 (2), 115–25.

Martin-Jones, D. (2006), *Deleuze, Cinema and National Identity: Narrative Time in National Contexts*, Edinburgh: Edinburgh University Press.

Pearlson, G. (2000), 'Neurobiology of schizophrenia', *Annals of Neurology*, 48 (4), 556–66.

Pisters, P. (2006), 'Arresting the flux of images and sounds: free indirect discourse and the dialectics of political cinema', in I. Buchanan and A. Parr (eds), *Deleuze and the Contemporary World*, Edinburgh: Edinburgh University Press, pp. 175–93.

Pisters, P. and Staat, W. (eds) (2005), *Shooting the Family: Transnational Media and Intercultural Values*, Amsterdam: Amsterdam University Press.

Williams, L. (1989), *Hard Core: Power, Pleasure and the Frenzy of the Visible*, Berkeley and Los Angeles: University of California Press.

Chapter 9

Bergson, H. (1971), *Time and Free Will: An Essay on the Immediate Data of Consciousness*, trans. F. L. Pogson, London: George Allen and Unwin.

Deleuze, G. (2000), 'The brain is the screen', in G. Flaxman, (ed.), *The Brain Is the Screen: Deleuze and the Philosophy of Cinema*, Minnesota and London: University of Minnesota Press, pp. 365–72.

Deleuze, G. (1998), 'To be done with judgement', in D. W. Smith (ed.), *Essays Critical and Clinical*, trans. D. W. Smith and M. A. Greco, Minneapolis: University of Minnesota Press, pp. 126–35.

Deleuze, G. and Guattari, F. (1991), *What Is Philosophy?*, trans. G. Burchell and H. Tomlinson, London: Verso.

Deleuze, G. and Guattari, F. (1988), *A Thousand Plateaus: Capitalism and Schizophrenia*, trans. B. Massumi, London: Continuum.

Deleuze, G. and Guattari, F. (1984), *Anti-Oedipus: Capitalism and Schizophrenia*, trans. R. Hurley, M. Seem and H. R. Lane, London: Continuum.

Dick, P. K. (1999), *A Scanner Darkly*, London: Gollancz.

Freud, S. (1991), 'The special characteristics of the system *Ucs*', in James Strachey (ed.), *PFL 11: On Metapsychology*, Harmondsworth: Penguin, pp. 167–222.

Guattari, F. (1995), *Chaosmosis: An Ethico Aesthetic Paradigm*, trans. P. Bains and J. Pefanis, Sydney: Power Publications.

Kennedy, B. M. (2000), *Deleuze and Cinema: The Aesthetics of Sensation*, Edinburgh: Edinburgh University Press.

Laplanche, J. and Pontalis, J. B. (1988), *The Language of Psychoanalysis*, London: Karnac.

Mulvey, L. (1975), 'Visual pleasure and narrative cinema', *Screen*, 16, 6–18.

Rushton, R. (2002), 'What can a face do? On Deleuze and faces', *Cultural Critique*, 51 (Spring), 219–37.

Chapter 10

Artaud, A. (1988), *Selected Writings*, trans. H. Weaver, Berkeley: University of California Press.

Canguilhem, G. (1991), 'The death of man, or exhaustion of cogito?', trans. C. Porter, in G. Gutting (ed.), *The Cambridge Companion to Foucault*, Cambridge: Cambridge University Press, pp. 71–91.

Deleuze, G. (1988), *Spinoza: Practical Philosophy*, trans. R. Hurley, San Francisco: City Lights Books.

Deleuze, G. and Guattari, F. (1999), *What Is Philosophy?*, trans. G. Burchell and H. Tomlinson, London and New York: Verso.

Deleuze, G. and Guattari, F. (1996), *Anti-Oedipus: Capitalism and Schizophrenia*, trans. R. Hurley, M. Seem and H. Lane, Minneapolis: University of Minnesota Press.

Deleuze, G. and Guattari, F. (1987), *A Thousand Plateaus: Capitalism and Schizophrenia*, trans. B. Massumi, London: Continuum.

Guattari, F. (2000), *The Three Ecologies*, trans. I. Pindar and P. Sutton, London: Continuum.

Guattari, F. (1996), *Soft Subversions*, trans. D. L. Sweet and C. Weiner. New York: Semiotext(e).

Guattari, F. (1995), *Chaosmosis: An Ethico Aesthetic Paradigm*, trans. P. Bains and J. Pefanis, Sydney: Powerhouse.

Hocquenghem, G. (1981), 'To destroy sexuality', trans. T. Gora, in S. Lotringer (ed.), *Polysexuality*, New York: Semiotext(e), pp. 260–64.

Serres, M. (2007), *The Parasite*, trans. L. R. Schehr, Minneapolis: University of Minnesota Press.

Serres, M. (2000), *The Birth of Physics*, trans. J. Hawkes, Manchester: Clinamen Press.

Index